RAF 'PLUMBER'

First published in 2006 by

WOODFIELD PUBLISHING
Bognor Regis, West Sussex, England
www.woodfieldpublishing.com

© Michael Anderton, 2006

All rights reserved.
No part of this publication may be reproduced
or transmitted in any form or by any means,
electronic or mechanical, nor may it be stored
in any information storage and retrieval system,
without prior permission from the publisher.

The right of Michael Anderton
to be identified as Author of this work
has been asserted in accordance with
the Copyright, Designs and Patents Act 1988

ISBN 1-84683-007-9

R.A.F. 'Plumber'

My 30 Years in the Armament Trade 1953-83

MICHAEL ANDERTON

Woodfield

*This book is dedicated to my family,
Pauline, Susan and Katie,
who persuaded me to put pen to paper.*

*But particularly to Pauline,
who shared the lifestyle we had while I was in the RAF
and helped me to remember many dates,
events and people for this book.*

Contents

Introduction .... *ii*
1. Early Connections 1
2. Halton 8
3. Tengah 20
4. Stafford 36
5. Safi 45
6. Eight Days from Malta 59
7. Bomb Disposal 67
8. Wildenrath 79
9. Coltishall 91
10. Akrotiri 98
11. Wattisham Lightnings 115
12. Wattisham Phantoms 125
13. Who needs a civvy armourer? 137
14. Epilogue 143
    Glossary *150*

Introduction

Firstly the title, you are probably wondering why the Royal Air Force (RAF) needs plumbers? Those of you in the know will be aware of the language of the armed services and in this case of the slang names for the various tradesmen that make up the highly specialised work force that provide the manpower in the Services.

Most of the terms are self-explanatory so 'Shinys' are the administrative staff, 'Snowdrops' the RAF police, 'Fairies' the instrument fitters, 'Sparkys' the electricians, 'Heavies' the engine fitters and so on. But where do the 'Plumbers' fit in? Somewhere back in history the business of servicing all those guns with their long tube-like barrels inevitably attracted the nickname of 'Plumbers'. In the RAF this was eventually applied to all aspects of the armament trade, from small arms, gun turrets, bombs, ejection seats, and all things that could go bang.

I was later to learn many more of these service names, 'Brats' were apprentices (to all except apprentices of course), 'Boggies' were National Servicemen, 'Matey-lots' were sailors and of course 'Pongos' were army personnel. Then going up a stage, 'Zobs' were officers, 'Brass' were senior officers and 'Steelies' were fighter pilots (steely-eyed killers).

I suppose I was always destined to be a plumber and looking back now I can see how the seeds were sown in my early days as a boy, and later in my teenage years. But it has done me no harm, as an armourer you become a Jack of all Trades. I have found that the experience of my thirty years service in the RAF has adequately equipped me with the ability to deal with most situations and fix almost anything that needs mending. In fact, when asked if I have a formal degree, I usually reply that I have a degree in the University of Life. I have found that experience far outweighs qualifications. The plumbing even continued after I left the RAF and my experience enabled me to undertake some real plumbing jobs such as installing two complete central heating systems.

~ RAF Plumber ~

In this book I have tried to portray my 30 years service in the RAF. Memories are often a little blurred and names, dates and events too easily forgotten. I have, therefore, done my best to use actual names but where necessary substitutes may be used. I have generally divided it up into chapters for each of my postings or sections of my life. If you find errors please forgive me, it is my story of what I think actually happened. If you find some of the terms confusing, I have added a Glossary at the end to list all the slang, abbreviations and technical terms used in the book.
Michael Anderton

1. Early Connections

When WWII started, I was only three years old and living with my parents at Little Wenham, a mediaeval settlement well off the beaten track and not even served by a public road. My early memories are of a happy, carefree life, involved with the local farm and the everyday life of the country. My father was not connected with farming; he was a Chartered Surveyor and worked in Ipswich for Garrod Turner Estate Agents, now known as Fenn Wright.

Author (front) and brother Peter at Oak Cottage, 1940.

As the war progressed it seems that my father was selected for, or volunteered to serve in, the Army – as leader of the secret local Underground Home Guard Unit and after training he was commissioned as a Captain. I remember going to Newark, staying in a bed and breakfast overnight, and watching my father's passing out parade at the nearby barracks. This must have been the start of my interest in the armed services.

The rest of the war years are rather a mish-mash of memories. My father would be out during all hours of the day and night training his 'guerrillas'. Meanwhile my mother was expected to transport arms, ammunition and rations to various underground bunkers, all concealed in her clothing or in my brother's pram. I can still visualise our front room at Oak Cottage; it was always full of guns, ammunition, grenades and other equipment awaiting distribution.

One day we were awakened in the middle of the night by someone knocking at the front door. The next morning I was introduced to our new guest, a RAF pilot who had been shot down, baled out and landed in the field next to our house. It was exciting to see his white parachute in a box by the front door, but very disappointing when he was collected by RAF transport, never to be seen again.

Author (right) and brother, 1942.

In London with Nannie, 1945.

But I had other contacts with the RAF to keep me interested. A good friend of my parents was Molly Pawsey, who was a commissioned WRAF officer. I don't know what work she did, but she was connected with RAF Martlesham and one day I was taken there on a visit. To my overwhelming delight, I was lifted up to the cockpit of a Spitfire and allowed to sit in the pilot's seat and hold the controls. What a joy for a small boy.

My maternal grandfather was an engineer and worked in the Ministry of Supply. We have since learned that he was connected with many secret projects, including Barnes Wallis and the bouncing bomb. My main recollections of him are of the interesting things he would have in his briefcase. A bomb release hook, an anti-saline cube for turning salt water into fresh, a luminous plate used in control rooms to mark controls during power failures, pieces of aircrew equipment and all sorts of objects. But best of all, he made model aircraft. He gave my brother and I Spitfires and Hurricanes, B17 bombers and all kinds of handmade toys. I even had a wooden model of the Big Bertha gun.

During this period, I also spent time in London with my paternal grandparents and witnessed V1 Doodlebugs, the blitz and the damage caused by V2 Rockets.

In 1942 the United States Army Air Force (USAAF) arrived at nearby Raydon and built an airfield to fly their P51 Mustangs and P47 Thunderbolts. Most of the domestic and technical areas were built in the adjoining parish of Great Wenham, where my boyhood friend Robin 'Dobby' Baldwin lived at Coopers Corner. I can clearly remember the sea of mud on the unmade roads during this construction period. Later, when flying got underway, the road to Bottle Bridge passed the end of the main runway, where an American serviceman in a Jeep controlled the traffic with green and red lamps as the aircraft came in to land. We all went to the old Capel St. Mary School and the Americans often took us there in their trucks while they were filling up their water bowsers from the brook at the end of the drive to Little Wenham Hall. Finally, I remember being taken up to the airfield for a Christmas party, a very exciting event for all of us young children.

In 1944, I was sent to Woodbridge School as a boarder and was, I believe, the youngest pupil there when I arrived. I hated it at first, but soon settled down to hold my own in the rough and tumble that inevitably happens at a boarding school. I have several memories of my time at Woodbridge, but as far as this story is concerned it was the war in the sky that was of concern. We spent many hours out on the playing fields and I can clearly recall seeing the fighter aircraft overhead dog fighting. We looked at the vapour trails (a twisted mass at times) and often found empty shell cases on the rugby and cricket pitches.

When the war ended, life returned to normal and I soon became involved again in the farming community. I joined the Young Farmers Club and became passionately interested in the mechanical side of the business. Even whilst attending Colchester Royal Grammar School I used any spare cash I had to buy copies of the

Farm Machinery Weekly and became familiar with all the latest mechanical trends. As I approached my 16th birthday I made my mind up that I wanted to be an agricultural engineer and become an apprentice at one of the major agricultural factories such as Ransoms Sims & Jefferies or Ernest Doe. But that was not to be, for although I made applications and went on interviews, there were many more boys than places available and I was inevitably turned down because I lived too far away from the works.

Capel St Mary School 1945 – author back row 5th from left.

This was in the days when National Service was still the norm and it was likely that at some stage I would probably have to serve my stint. It was at this time that a friend of the family who had been in the RAF during the war suggested that I join as a RAF Apprentice. My parents had divorced by now and my mother, struggling to look after three growing boys on very little money, was keen to get me settled into something. We had to move from Oak Cottage and the best accommodation she could find was a tiny crossing cottage at Little Wenham, on the old Bentley-to-Hadleigh branch line.

The Gatehouse – Little Wenham.

Enquiries about the RAF were made and an application form obtained. This revealed that an entrance exam was required and, because I had left Colchester Royal Grammar School, aged 16, with no qualifications, it was decided that some extra tuition was required to bring me up to the required standard. I eventually took the exam at the old Labour Exchange in Rope Walk, Ipswich (now the home of the Registrar) and waited for the results.

I duly learnt that I had managed to attain the standard required and the next step was to travel to RAF Halton in Buckinghamshire to attend the selection board. This, of course, was quite an adventure for a country boy, but as I had plenty of experience travelling on my own by train during the war it was easy. The route from Ipswich to Halton was via Liverpool Street and Baker Street Stations to Wendover. On the train I met up with others on their way to the selection board. From Wendover we were taken by bus to a barrack block at RAF Halton and given our first taste of RAF life. The main thing I remember was the food. I had never experienced plastic eggs or large china mugs of tea, but it was all an exciting new experience for us. I met up with a lad from Norfolk, Graham Napthan, and we became quite good friends. The selection process consisted of medical tests, aptitude tests and visits to the various workshops, all designed to enable us to pick the trade we would like to train in. I had always thought that to train as an electrician would be a useful attribute when I eventually returned to civvy street, but alas this was not to be. I was advised that there were no vacancies for electricians. I could be either an engine fitter or an armourer. I had been full of wonder when visiting the armament workshop, lined with gun-turrets, bombs and various armament equipment, and for some reason or other I opted for that.

Armament Workshop - RAF Halton 1953

We all returned on the train after a couple of days of this routine, wondering if, and when, we would meet up again. Graham and I travelled home from Liverpool Street on the same train, he continuing on to Diss after I got off at Ipswich.

2. Halton

After a few days I received a letter informing me of the date when I was to join up and eventually travelled to RAF Halton again to start my initial training. Our intake was the 74th Entry and we were based in No.1 Wing. First we had to swear our allegiance to the new Queen and then sign on the dotted line. My date of enlistment was 28 April 1953, three months before my 17th birthday. I was allocated my new Service Number – 588577 – quite an easy one to remember, but not as easy as my friend Graham, who got 588588. We were all paraded outside the barrack block we had been allocated and were given the Queen's shilling. As an Anderton, my name was high on the alphabetical list and when my name was called I had to shout 'Sir! 577' – the 'last three' of my new number.

One by one, everyone's name was called and this became an opportunity for nicknames to be invented. My nickname, 'Andy', would stick with me throughout my service career, although outside the RAF, family and friends have always used my Christian name, or variations on it. My friend Graham with a name like Napthan (naphthalene) became 'Mothballs', Richard Minors-Wallis was 'Shotgun' (double-barrelled), two red-headed lads became 'Big Ginge' and 'Little Ginge', and so it went on… There were one or two colonial lads joining up with us and everyone had difficulty with the name of a lad from Ceylon, Abeygunawardena, which was soon shortened to 'Abbey' and of course a lad from New Zealand had to be 'Kiwi'.

Next on the agenda was the issuing of kit. Although we had received no drill instruction, we were formed up in three ranks and marched off, a shambling mass, to the stores. We were still in our civvies, of course, but the NCOs in charge shouted and bellowed instructions in an effort to teach us the basic art of marching. At the stores we were all measured by the tailor, who shouted out a variety of numbers to the airmen behind the long counter. We then all passed down the aisle, catching various pieces of clothing and equipment that were flung at us, including two sets of uniform, a kit bag and two greatcoats. On the way back to the barrack block we were loaded down with all this kit and it was impossible to even try and be smart and orderly. Finally, we were all marched off to the barber to receive a one-off free regulation-style haircut, known as a 'short back and sides'. Later this would become known to me as 'getting your head sharpened' – a term used throughout the armed services. One of the funny things about the services is that although everything is provided free of charge, you do have to pay for a haircut. Some wag once suggested that as it grew in service time, a haircut should be free. But of course the response from authority was that some of it grew during off duty time, to which the counter response was that you only had the hair that grew during duty time cut off!

Next we were photographed ready for the issue of our 1250s. A RAF Form 1250 is the standard service identity card that we would carry and be called upon to show regularly throughout our service careers. It practically became part of your person, to the extent that when I finally left the RAF I got one of the new photo driving licences just to satisfy my need to be able to identify myself.

The 74th Entry 1953 – Author front row 5th from left.

Back at the barrack block we were given instructions on how to look after our kit and prepare it for kit inspection. A photograph of what it should look like was posted on the notice board and a time for inspection that only gave us a few hours to prepare. This was a routine that would stay with us for our three years at Halton, and once the shortcuts to a good layout were learned, it all seemed quite easy. But many of the chores associated with the 'Bull' were really tiresome. This included spit and polish of boots, the need to always have sharp creases in our uniform, making up bed packs every morning, the incessant polishing of the linoleum floor and room jobs. These were the everyday cleaning and polishing tasks that had to be done and were shared out amongst all of us in a weekly rota.

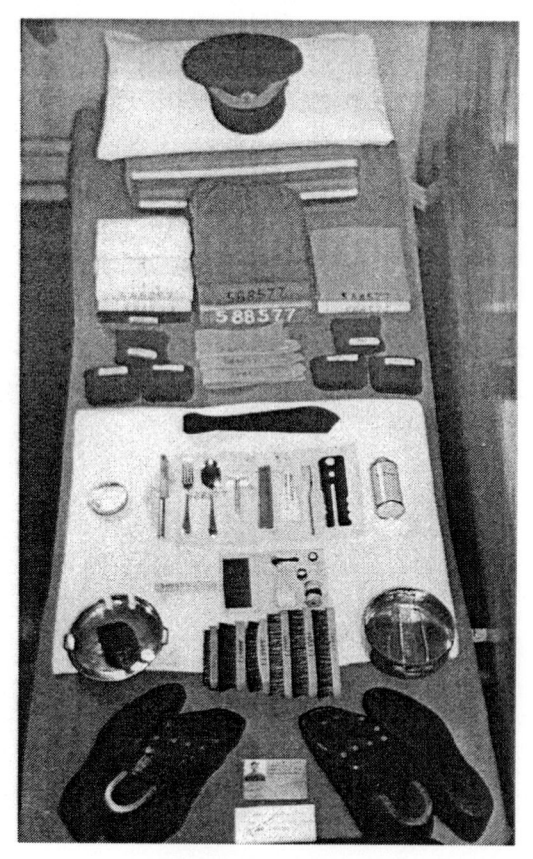

Author's kit inspection.

As soon as we had mastered the uniform and its many parts, it was time for 'square bashing'. Initially this consisted of a solid two weeks of drill to get us into some sort of cohesive unit. It is surprising how long it takes to instinctively turn right or left on command. It looks quite comical when you see a squad at drill and one poor soul turns the opposite way to everyone else. But in the services it is always the same and you all just keep at it until everyone has mastered the idea. Of course, the drill instructors did plenty of shouting and a Sergeant Davis in particular always shouted, 'What have you got at the end of your arm lad, a bunch of bananas? Clench your fists!' Later in the programme we were instructed in the drill associated with the Lee Enfield rifle and the many intricate moves that it introduced to our movements.

After two weeks of drill, with instructors bawling and shouting at us all day, it was time to start our technical training, the first phase of which is called 'basic'. For the next three years our flight would form up at 0800 hours every morning on the road outside our barrack block and march down to the workshops. On the way we would join up with all the other flights and the apprentice pipe band in a long chain of humanity moving from the domestic site to the technical or education sites. The senior entry was always allowed to be the first flight behind the band, whilst us mere juniors brought up the rear in descending seniority. At lunchtimes we would march back up the hill again, have our meal, and then at a set time march back down the hill. Finally, at 1700 hours it would be the last march up the hill for tea and all the other evening duties or pastimes.

One of the major entertainment opportunities in the evenings (when we had spare time) was to visit the Astra Cinema to see the latest offering; the programme was usually changed every two days. But with very limited cash available it was essential to get into the cheapest seats to avoid the higher prices of 1 shilling (5p) and upwards. Tickets for the seats in the first few rows were sold at a special door at the side of the building for 6d (2½p). There was such a demand for these seats that we rushed to get a place at the front of the queue in order to get in. There were even railings each side of the door to keep us in an orderly queue, but inevitably there were many others with the same idea. The heaving mass was known as the 'tanner crush', for obvious reasons. But on one occasion I did get in for nothing and that was when the coronation of Queen Elizabeth II was shown on the big screen.

The Basic Phase taught us all about hand tools and their practical uses. This was partly a classroom lecture but mainly bench work, completing various test jobs. At a very early stage we were given a piece of mild steel, required to cut slots in it with a hacksaw, chisel all the strips off and then file it flat to within one thousandth of an inch accuracy. By the time you had mastered that, you probably had very sore and bleeding knuckles but were very proficient at filing a piece of mild steel flat.

Once we had mastered the use of hand tools we moved on to the more interesting phases of small arms, bombs, pyrotechnics, ejection seats, gun turrets, bomb carriers, bomb trolleys, explosives, rockets and all the things that the RAF use that go bang. These 'phases', as they were known, continued throughout our three years at Halton, all mainly conducted in the armament workshops and with a variety of civilian and service instructors.

Not all of our training was on armament equipment. Half our time was spent in 'Schools', sitting in classrooms just like any other technical college. Schools were a separate set of buildings, where Education Officers or civilian teachers, usually ex-RAF personnel, instructed us. There was homework to be done in off duty times, just to keep the pressure on, and I suppose to keep us out of mischief. We did all the usual subjects like English and Maths, but much of the Science was centred on subjects such as electricity, trajectories, the chemistry of explosives and general physics, etc. All, of course, were connected with our particular trades and to prepare us all for the final goal of passing out as fully qualified Junior Technicians (J/T).

We were in the middle of the Blacksmith and Sheet Metalwork phase when I reported sick with a pain in my groin. This was diagnosed by the Medical Officer (MO) as a hernia and within a few days I was in hospital having an operation. Princess Mary's RAF Hospital was handily part of RAF Halton and I had ten days of lying in bed with no marching up and down the hill. Finally, I was given a railway warrant and a Form 295 (leave pass) for 14 days sick leave at home. Then it was back to the training. Luckily my break hadn't interfered too much with my training and I was not required to go back an entry to make up for the loss of time.

Occasionally, we went on external visits. The most memorable one for me being a day trip to the Martin Baker ejection seat factory at Denham in Buckinghamshire. As plumbers it would be our job to fit and remove the seats from aircraft and to undertake the very exacting task of servicing the various components to ensure proper operation. At the factory we were shown around the works, given lunch, shown films and finally each of us who volunteered were allowed to have a ride on the test rig. We were strapped into an ejection seat mounted on a near vertical rail on the back of a lorry. The seat ejection gun had been loaded with the low powered explosive cartridges that are used to operate the seat and when all was ready we were allowed to pull the face blind handle over our faces to operate the rig. This is an experience I shall never forget and when later in my career I would talk to pilots who had ejected in seats that I had fitted or serviced, I knew exactly what they felt like at the time. Before we left the factory we were given Martin Baker ashtrays and a brochure describing how the seat worked. The ashtray still has pride of place in my home today.

The most exciting phase of our training was 'Airfields' when we would do our training on real aircraft on the airfield. This was the chance to have a go at removing and replacing aircraft guns, loading ammunition (dummy) into gun turrets, fitting ejection seats and experiencing live ground firing of aircraft guns. But the real prize was to be issued with a shiny black waterproof mackintosh. This was the ultimate badge of seniority, for it was only when you reached senior entry status that you undertook the Airfield Phase. And because it was a longer distance to march to the airfield each day, it was deemed fitting that we had proper waterproofs to wear. All apprentices were issued with a groundsheet cape, the only piece of waterproof clothing provided. As we marched up and down to the workshops or schools everyday we had to carry our groundsheets, rolled up and worn bandoleer fashion across the body. It was such a relief to have the black 'Mac' to distinguish us from everyone else and prove that we were the senior entry. Whilst on Airfields I had my first flight in an aircraft, an elderly Dragon Rapide came in especially to take us up in batches of nine for what is called an air experience flight. It only lasted about 10 minutes but as it was the first time it was a very exciting moment. Also while we were on the Airfields Phase an experimental Fairey Rotodyne came in to land. This unusual machine was a cross between an autogyro, a helicopter and a turboprop jet. The most striking thing was the tremendous noise that came from the ramjets on the tips of the blades.

In the early stages of training we were not allowed off camp, but after getting our uniform and completing the initial square-bashing phase, we were allowed out for limited periods. At first these meant visits to the Toc H Club in Wendover, but later we managed trips to Aylesbury and beyond. Money was always a problem, pay was set at 17/6d (75p) per week of which 10/- (50p) went into your POSB (Post Office Savings Bank or Pos-Bee) account and 7/6d (25p) paid out in cash. This severely limited our activities and only allowed the occasional evening out. After initial training we were allowed 36-hour passes. This meant we could leave camp from midday on Saturday to 2359 hours on Sunday. I was able to use this time to hitchhike home for an overnight stay and a few hours socialising with my friends and then, after lunch on Sunday, head off back to arrive in good time before lights out. In those days hitchhiking was easy with a uniform on and everyone accepted that servicemen had little money. But there were some peculiar people on the roads and one had to be careful about the propositions that were suggested. Once a month we were eventually allowed 48-hour passes allowing us to leave on Friday evening and return on Sunday night.

At the age of 17½ we were given a pay rise and received the princely sum of 49/- (£2.45) a week rising at 18 years of age to 56/- (£2.80) a week. If I recall we were only given around £1 of this at pay parade, the rest went into our POSB account. Our POSB books were kept until the end of term when they would be handed out ready for us to go on leave. We also received our pay and ration allowances the day before we left and it was probably the only time we ever had any money. The problem was that many of us borrowed money during the term and this had to be paid back at this time which often left us in the situation of going home nearly broke. Luckily, we were also given a return train ticket home and, together with our leave pass, at least we got away for a short break and the chance to wear civvies at home.

A day out in London

As we commenced our last year of training we went on summer camp to RAF Woodvale near Southport. We were to be living under canvas for two weeks. We left very early one morning with our kit packed in backpacks to march to Tring Station. I suppose we needed to leave early to march the five miles to the station in time for the special train. It was, however, a very relaxed march and we were even allowed to sing on the route when we were away from the houses. At the camp on the airfield it was what we expected, field kitchens, bucket toilets, sleeping in tents and all good fun as long as it didn't rain. We soon got to know when the man came to empty the toilets as the smell was really dreadful. He soon got crudely nicknamed the 'Turd Burglar'.

Summer Camp – Author centre front

There were no aircraft based at Woodvale except a Spitfire that took off every day to do a weather reconnaissance flight. But the runway was used for circuits and bumps by other aircraft and Meteors and Canberras were often seen. We had a full programme of long marches, field exercises by day and by night and sporting events to keep us busy. In the evenings and weekend we were occasionally allowed off the camp and usually made our way to Ainsdale Station to catch the train to Southport. We also had another taste of flying. An Avro Anson came in one day and took us on trips around the area. The trip I went on was to Blackpool to fly around the tower and return. The culmination of the two weeks was a big daytime exercise in the sand dunes between the railway and the sea. We were all split up into different groups of attackers and defenders, issued with our rifles and several rounds of blank ammunition and told the rules of the game. It was all good fun as long as everyone kept to the rules and played dead or injured when they had been shot. At midday we all had our pack lunches in the sand dunes before commencing again in the afternoon. After an hour or so the Instructors started walking around blowing whistles and telling us the exercise had been called to halt and we were all to head back to the camp. That evening we were told that some fool had been firing off live ammunition during the day and although no one had been shot, the exercise was abandoned for safety reasons. Who was firing the live rounds and where they had got it from we were never told.

Sgt Apprentice Anderton – 3 Wing RAF Halton

Finally, we approached the time for our graduation parade. Exams had to be taken and passed in order to complete the training and those who had qualified were able to go on the parade. The 28th March 1956 was the great day when we became fully qualified J/Ts. Every trainee on the station took part in the parade, watched by parents, friends and dignitaries. As the senior entry graduating, our two flights escorted the Queen's Colour in quick and slow march-pasts, accompanied by the brass and pipe bands, whilst everyone else looked on. As a Sergeant Apprentice I was given the role of No. 2 Flight Marker, a task that entailed considerable responsibility. I was the individual that everyone else aimed on for their distance and spacing. The parade culminated in the Advance in Review Order and General Salute, an impressive manoeuvre when everyone on the parade marches forward a set number of paces, halts and completes a general salute to the reviewing officer. Once we were dismissed it was time for the apprentices' tradition of removing our hats and en masse throwing them into the air.

74th Entry Passing Out parade, General Salute

We were now fully qualified and the very first thing to do was to get our new J/T badges sewn on to our uniforms. I was very lucky that my mother had managed to get to Halton for the day and she was able to come back to my bunk (room) in the barrack block. There she was finally able to sew on my single upside-down stripes and remove the brass apprentice wheel badge and sergeant apprentice stripes. As my posting was to be RAF Tengah in Singapore, and I would not be leaving until May, I was able to leave most of my kit at Halton until after my leave. I would be spending a few more days here before the posting overseas took effect. As for Mothballs

(Graham) he got a UK posting and I never met up with him again until after I had left the service. But Shotgun (Richard Minors-Wallis) had also got a posting to Tengah and with a few others from the 74th Entry we would travel there together.

Returning to Halton as a J/T now on pay of £5-5s (£5.25) a week I really felt I had made progress in the world. But for a few days those of us due to go abroad were put into a group of nomads with not a lot to do. Every morning for a few weeks we would be given jobs to do around the station, but these were comparatively easy and most afternoons were spent in the local café or in bed sleeping. However, in early May we moved out and left by train for RAF Innsworth in Gloucestershire.

3. Tengah

RAF Innsworth was the place where all personnel were prepared for despatch to their various overseas postings. As soon as we arrived we were split up into groups and merged with other groups of airmen all heading for various destinations. I was put in the Far East group and we went through the routine of tropical kit issue, some lectures on sexual diseases and other health matters and then jabbed up to the eyeballs with inoculations.

Having completed that phase in the first two days, we were bussed off to RAF Clyffe Pypard in Wiltshire. It was 8 May 1956. This was to be our transit camp stopover for the night. Early next morning after breakfast we were back on the bus but this time for the short distance to RAF Lyneham. The RAFs fleet of Hastings transport aircraft was based here and we were to be flown out to RAF Changi in Singapore. However, the aircraft only flew during daylight hours and due to the low speed of travel and the route taken, it would take us five days to get there.

We took off from the long runway and noisily lumbered into the air. In those days transport aircraft could hardly be called comfortable. The seats were mainly canvas and under each one was a Mae West inflatable jacket in case we came down in the drink, and a cardboard box filled with a packed lunch for the day. But we were all brave young men off on a big adventure and it was all so exciting. In-flight drinks were sparingly dispensed by the Air QuarterMaster from large Thermos flasks and cardboard cups and we settled down for our first hop to RAF Idris in Libya.

Our flight lasted around six hours I believe and it was quite a change to land in the warmth and palm trees of North Africa. But it was a quick meal, beer in the NAAFI, buy some souvenirs and bed for the night ready to start the routine again the next day. The second leg of our trip would be to RAF Habbaniya in Iraq. Our stay here was really awful, the mess tent was all sand and flies, with weevils in the bread and our sleeping accommodation turned out to be a six man tent in the sand with duck boards on the floor. We were very pleased to get away from there; our third day would take us to Pakistan and RAF Mauripur near Karachi.

Hastings at IWM Duxford

We landed in the early evening and before being able to disembark the passenger compartment of the aircraft was thoroughly sprayed with fly spray by a local. On the bus trip to the transit accommodation we saw the need for all the fly spray. Dotted along the roads were old oil drums burning with black smoke pouring out of the tops. We were told that this is how the locals disposed of their toilet waste. The transit rooms were unbearably hot and we were pleased when the sun rose the next morning and we managed to get away from that dreadful place. Flying on from Mauripur our next port of call would be Ceylon and RAF Negombo. Now here was a place that we really enjoyed. It was tropical but not too hot, and the accommodation was just fine, we even got to buy pineapples from the locals. If this was a taste of the Far East let's get on with our journey. Our final leg was across the Indian Ocean to RAF Changi on Singapore Island. Some of our party would continue on to Hong Kong but for me it was the end of an interesting journey halfway around the world.

The RAF transport took us across the island to RAF Tengah where I would be spending the next 2½ years. At that time it was the height of the Malayan emergency and Tengah was home to New Zealand, Australian and UK Squadrons operating against the communists in the jungles of Malaya. This meant I was now on active service and after 24 hours on the station was entitled to the General Service Medal (GSM) with Malaya clasp. No 1B Royal Australian Air Force (RAAF) Squadron were operating Lincoln bombers, an enlarged version of the Lancaster, No.14 Royal New Zealand Air Force (RNZAF) Squadron were flying Venom Mk 4 fighter bombers and No.60 RAF Squadron also flying Venom Mk 4 fighter bombers.

I was allocated a bed space in Learoyd Block in a barrack room full of other plumbers. This was the closest barrack block to the main runway, so close in fact that the Air Traffic Control (ATC) section was situated on the roof. It was a bit spartan with only cold water showers and during the monsoon season the high winds often blew rain through the glassless windows and shutters. But otherwise it was quite comfortable with a Malay bearer (servant) called Douglas who did all the cleaning and a little Chinese lady called Lucy who did sewing for a small fee. I soon settled in and completed my arrival procedure. This required me to book in at Station Headqarters (SHQ) where I was given an arrival chit. This was standard procedure on arrival at all RAF stations and consisted of a card with spaces for many different sections such as clothing store, pay section, place of work etc. that one had to visit to get the card signed and be registered as a new member of the station staff.

On the first day of work, I went down to the Station Armament Headquarters with all the other lads and after a tour of the sections there I was allocated a job working in the Aircraft Servicing Section (ASF). The ASF armament section was situated in one of the main hangers where I joined a small team of plumbers. Our corporal-in-charge was a New Zealander and with him were two RNZAF Leading Aircraftsmen (LAC) armament fitters a RAF Senior Aircraftsman (SAC) armament mechanic and myself. The team was responsible for all the second line servicing of RAF and RNZAF Venom aircraft on the station. The RAAF did all their own servicing in a separate hanger and we had little contact with them. Our task was to carry out all the Venom's servicing procedures and testing of the armament systems. This included removal, fitting and arming of ejection seats, removal, fitting and harmonisation of the four 20 mm guns, removal, fitting and testing of the bomb release and rocket launch equipment and all the other armament related parts of the aircraft.

Venom FB4 – ASF RAF Tengah 1956

I was put to work with one of the RNZAF LAC fitters who happened to be a Scotsman that had signed up after immigrating to New Zealand. He showed me the ropes and after a few days I was working on my own from the servicing schedules. The first time I armed an ejection seat was quite a scary moment. But it taught me to be meticulous in my work, because mistakes in this trade could mean the end of someone's life, including my own. It was at this time that I learnt the saying 'Never assume, check' a phrase that I fortunately stuck to throughout my service career.

One day we had a rather light-hearted but dangerous moment. The Venom has two pylons under the wings to carry bombs and on each wing tip are fuel tanks. On the cockpit floor either side of the ejection seat are two handles to manually jettison either the bombs from the pylons or the wing tip tanks in cases of emergency. These are tested by fitting weights to the release hooks and pulling the levers up. One day, in the busy hanger, there was a very loud crash from one of the aircraft that was up on jacks and aircraft fuel was seen to be running across the floor. All went very quiet and after a few seconds a head popped up above the cockpit canopy rails and a plumber (not me) who shall remain nameless said in a dejected voice 'Oh dear I seem to have pulled the wrong one'. Luckily the wing tip fuel tanks were not completely full and the only damage was to the tanks that are designed to be jettisoned anyway.

After three months working in ASF I was promoted to corporal and moved to the Bomb Dump where I became NCO in charge (i/c) of No.1 shift. Practically every day the two Venom and one Lincoln squadrons were carrying out strikes or training over the jungles of Malaya and the Bomb Dump was the place where all the bombs, rockets and ammunition came from. That meant we were kept very busy hence the reason why there were two shifts of personnel to supply the armament stores to the squadrons at all hours. One shift would start at 0700 hours every morning and work until 1230 hours. The other shift would then take over until 1900 hours then be on standby during the night if required. The shifts would take it in turns to work at weekends from 0700 to 1900 hours on Saturday and Sunday. This meant that we had every other weekend off. During a week of early shifts we would have the afternoon off or if we were on the late shift a lay in until lunchtime. This was to be my working routine for the next two years.

Each shift consisted of six men, all RAF plumbers except one chap I had on my shift who was in the RNZAF. However, he was a Manxman so was quite at home working with the Brits, the others being a mix of National Service and Regular armament mechanics. We also had a gang of about twelve local labourers that we called coolies, a mixture of Malays, Indians and Chinese headed by a charge hand we called Sailor. They worked six days a week from 0700 to 1800 hours and were a great bunch of very reliable workers. Many of them had been working in the bomb dump for so long that they were trusted to work unsupervised and often knew more about the job than we did. Running the whole show was Warrant Officer (WO) Mick Game, Sgt Jock Wilson and an airman in the office, whilst a national service J/T ran the Ground Equipment section. A national service J/T was a rarity but this chap had a degree in engineering to justify it!

The Coolies and part of No.2 Shift – Bomb Dump RAF Tengah

Life was never dull with the regular deliveries of bombs, rockets and ammunition into the dump from the maintenance unit (MU) at RAF Seleter all delivered by the lorry load. Then the never-ending flow of prepared stores for the operational squadrons being delivered out across the airfield using our two David Brown and one Fordson Major tractors. Our time was spent fusing up trolley loads of bombs, assembling three-inch rockets and man-handling boxes and boxes of 20 mm and .5 inch ammunition. This would all be delivered to the respective squadrons ready for the squadron plumbers to load onto the aircraft. By far the biggest users were the Australians in terms of tons of bombs. The Lincoln bomber is similar to the Lancaster and carried a bomb load of fourteen 1000lb bombs. There were about ten aircraft on the squadron and this meant that they could use a considerable number of bombs on a 'strike' over the jungle. We delivered the bombs on Type F bomb trolleys, each trolley carried four bombs and were towed by one of our tractors. It was usual practice to have ready prepared on trolleys at least one complete load of bombs for each aircraft so that whenever called upon we could make an immediate issue to the squadrons.

RAF Tengah Bomb Dump 1957

The bomb dump covered several acres with rubber and banana trees scattered around and was built on a hill with a one-way road all around linking the various storage bays, preparation sheds, storage sheds and workshops. It was possible to tow a train of about twelve empty trolleys around this road although when towing live loads it would be reduced to about six for safety and to negotiate the hill out of the dump gates. The trains of ready fused bombs would be stored on the road all linked together and ready for issue. Trolley loads of rockets all armed with their 60lb High Explosive (HE) or Semi Armour Piercing (SAP) warheads would also be ready positioned for immediate issue when the call came from operations. We also prepared 500lb bombs and 25lb smoke and flash practice bombs, maintaining stocks of these also in readiness. One unusual feature of the bomb dump was the fire alarm bells dotted around the access roads. These were made from half 500lb bomb casings with a striker made from a bomb pistol (fuze) hanging on a rope in the centre. The local story was that some time in the recent past the communist terrorists had infiltrated during the night and sawn the bombs in half to steal the high explosives inside. The casings had been found in the rubber trees some time later and used for fire bells. How true this was I never found out but one of the duties of the NCO i/c the duty shift was to count all the bombs in the open storage bays every night and morning in case there were any missing.

The work of preparing or fusing so many bombs was quite a slick operation that at times may have appeared dangerous. The fusing shed was set between blast walls and had double doors at each end so that trolley loads of bombs could be towed through. As each load arrived the boys on the shift set to removing blanking plugs, fitting detonators, pistols, tail units and fitting all the safety devices. As NCO i/c I supervised, recorded all the details in a log and painted the serial numbers and other information on each bomb. Everyone knew exactly what to do, but one or two characters needed special attention. Our New Zealand friend 'Manx' was sometimes a bit heavy handed and I often had to caution him about it. He just loved to fit the sensitive detonators and conical support springs to the front and rear cavities of the bombs but occasionally would drop them and one time even trod on one. Needless to say, I kept him away from that job unless it was urgent.

Although each trolley of bombs was supposed to stop inside the fusing shed as we worked on it, often there was not time to do this. A six-trolley train of bombs would be halted with the centre trolleys in the shed while everyone set to work on the complete train even though four of the trolleys were not quite within the confines of the blast walls. This certainly speeded up the job and was justified as an operational necessity to keep the supply of weapons flowing to the squadrons.

The whole of this area was on a slope and on one occasion I needed a wheel chock for one of the trolleys to enable us to unhitch the tractor. I turned to Sailor the charge hand of the coolies and asked him to fetch one. He went off and a few seconds later we heard an awful grinding crashing noise and a few thuds. It seems he walked down the road and had taken a chock from one of the trains of six-trolley loads of fused bombs on the side of the road.

Fusing Shed and 1000lb HE bombs ready to go

Usually there were several chocks preventing the loads rolling down the hill but on this occasion it was the only one left. The train of bombs had rolled down the hill with the towbar scraping on the road and gradually crossing the road as it went. The towbar had buried itself in the roadside bank and thrown the four bombs onto the road. On the second trolley all the bombs had shot forward and were at different angles in the wreckage. All the other bombs in the train had shifted forward and we had to get the whole lot sorted out quickly and without a fuss. All the coolies and my shift of plumbers mucked in and we man-handled the 1000lb bombs back onto their respective undamaged trolleys in the correct positions. There were a few damaged tail fins, locking pins and minor fitments that we changed, but the remainder just needed a good clean up and a bit of paint here and there before we towed them back into the storage position, this time with plenty of chocks under the wheels. Although it was a frightening situation, it proved how well the safety devices on a live bomb protect it from accidental detonation.

A present for the communists in the jungle

Another incident that also proved this point occurred whilst the RAAF plumbers were loading bombs on the Lincolns for a strike later in the day. A call came in asking for a plumber to go over and give them a hand because there was a problem. As the senior person on duty at the time I jumped on a tractor and went over to where they were working just down the road. To load the aircraft with fourteen 1000lb bombs the loaded trolleys are positioned under the bomb bay. The bombs are then winched up to the bomb carriers in the roof of the bomb bay and a bomb latched onto each bomb hook before being crutched (tightened). Continuity safety checks are then carried out on the bomb release circuits of the bomb carrier and aircraft and then the empty trolleys are pulled out and returned to the bomb dump. Unfortunately, there had either been a fault in the circuit or someone had used the wrong switches, but all fourteen bombs had been released and crashed down onto the trolleys below. Although the bomb casings were intact, many of the tail units were badly damaged, but worst of all, some of the pistols in the bomb noses had struck the trolley cross-members and sheared off, exposing the sensitive detonators. It was my task to defuse all the damaged bombs, including removing damaged bits of pistols and safety devices, before removing the detonators. The whole load was eventually returned to the bomb dump where we reused most of the undamaged parts. Luckily, no one was injured and it was put down to just another operational incident.

Another Venom FB4 nose wheel collapse

Occasionally, the Malayan Emergency produced a state of panic when excessive amounts of explosive stores were required for an offensive in the jungle and it was beyond one bomb shift to cope with the situation. Personnel from the Station Armament Headquarters would come and work in the bomb dump overnight as labourers, or for however long it took to get everything prepared and issued. We often worked through the night in the sticky heat, fusing bombs, assembling three-inch rockets and issuing boxes of ammunition. One evening while there was just my bomb shift on duty we had the Aussies waiting for their bomb loads to be delivered. Suddenly they arrived at the bomb dump gates with their tractors. 'Where are our bombs you Pommy bastards' they shouted in a very unfriendly way and forgetting how I had helped them out in the past. But we didn't take it too seriously, life was just too hectic to worry about it.

Singapore was a great place to spend our spare time. I was a single corporal with a bit of spare cash and could afford a few luxuries. On promotion I was entitled to my own bunk, as it is known. I had started to get interested in jazz while at Halton and was now able to start a record collection. On visits to Singapore City I would spend many a happy hour browsing through the records in the air-conditioned shops for the latest Gerry Mulligan, Dave Brubeck or such like record. I still have my collection today and still like jazz. I also bought myself a nice record player that I later upgraded to a proper Hi Fi system including a tape recorder and started to have contact with other jazz enthusiasts. The opportunity came up for me to do a jazz hour on Radio Tengah broadcasting on the internal station tannoy system from a room on the top floor of SHQ. From this I developed a weekly one hour jazz request show that I called 'Nights at the Turntable' after my signature tune, a record by Gerry Mulligan of the same name that has always been my favourite. My friends and I occasionally managed to get across to RAF Changi where the Far East Air Force (FEAF) Band had a weekly jazz club of all live music. That really was one of the special days out when my pal Ben Britain would hire a car for the day and we would go for a meal down town or a swim in the sea before the club visit. As a result of my possession of a tape recorder I was able to help a small group of lads practice their singing/guitar group routines before they performed live on Radio Singapore. That group was led by Keith Barron and later became known as the Barron Knights who, as far as I know, are still performing today.

One happy event was when my pal Shotgun got married. He had been courting a girl called Valerie at Halton and while at Tengah he made arrangements for her to travel to Singapore on a troopship as family. On arrival they were married in the station church at RAF Tengah and then moved into a flat down town. I was his best man and it was a grand occasion to get dressed up for a party. This was to be the first of several times that I took on best man duties for various people during my service and a task at which I became quite proficient.

I was also able to meet my younger brother Peter who had joined the Navy also as an Armourer, or Ordnance Artificer as they called them. He was on his way to his new ship HMS Rotoriti and had flown out from the UK and was stopping over a few days in HMS Terror, the local Naval Base. I got permission to take him to RAF Tengah where I found a bed for him. He stayed a few days with me and it made a nice change to have contact with my family. I also had my 21st birthday at Tengah. I recall my mother sending me a pair of gold cuff links, but the £5 note my uncle sent was confiscated by the Customs, mainly because there was a currency restriction in force and he had declared it on the envelope.

Being on shift work there was always plenty to do at RAF Tengah during our time off. If we weren't in the NAAFI drinking large quantities of Tiger Beer, we would be at the swimming pool just relaxing, keeping cool and having fun or at the Astra Cinema. Then there would be visits to Tengah village where there was an array of local shops where you could buy all manner of electrical and luxury goods and even get a suit made in a couple of days. Before I left Singapore I had two suits made ready for my return to UK. And of course there was the inevitable bar where we spent many a happy hour testing the various combinations of alcoholic drinks or even iced tea and coffee if we had had a bad night the previous evening. It was here that I learned to like whisky, originally with lemonade but later neat or with ice. There were also other places to go, often a bar that the Brits frequented, but also interesting places like the Tiger Balm Gardens, Kranji War Cemetery, across the Causeway to Malaya to Jahore Buru and various places around Singapore City.

The Station Photography Section was situated in the Station Armament Headquaters building and this was a very useful source of information. Inevitably with so much flying activity going on there were regular incidents such as aircraft running off the runway and more serious crashes where aircraft were written off. The station photographers were always quickly brought onto the scene and this provided a great source of interesting photographs and information. There were no security restrictions in those days and I still have an album full of these official photographs. I have pictures of aircraft in all sorts of states of wreckage, some aerial shots of bombing over Malaya and formation flying for displays. Some more serious incidents were also recorded such as an aircraft crashing into a row of married quarters and a tree falling on the detonator store in the bomb dump. Because we were in the nearest barrack block to the runway we always had a grandstand view of any incidents that occurred on the airfield and our friendly photographers were able to supply the pictures.

One particularly interesting trip I managed to get on was a flight up to RAF Butterworth in one of the RAAF Lincolns. There were four of us and we were all kitted out with parachutes ready for the flight. During take off we had to sit on the floor of the aircraft, but once we were airborne we were able to wander around inside the fuselage. We took it in turns riding in the various gun turrets and bomb aimer's positions for the trip 'up country'. At Butterworth we went for a look around the Station Armament Section and then on for lunch in the Airmen's Mess. The return trip was very similar and I was able to take photographs as souvenirs. This was the only time I was able to leave Singapore Island during my time there, although others managed to get to Hong Kong by taking leave and travelling to HK and back on the troopships that had spare capacity.

Even though it is nearly 50 years since I experienced Singapore I still have many vivid memories of my time there. Just for the record I will list some of the things that others who were there at the time will remember. Taxi dancing, Boogie Street, sing songs with the Navy in the Britannia Club, the Chinese habit of spitting through bus windows, pick-up taxis, falling in monsoon drains and monsoon weather, Spam fritters, bananas with everything, Malayan language phrases such as pergi lekas (go quickly) and many, many more. I particularly remember the Chinese had a habit of calling everyone John. Every morning the NAAFI van arrived at the Bomb Dump and a little Chinese man would open up the rear and greet us with 'You want egg loll today John' much to everyone's merriment.

A trip to RAF Butterworth in a RAAF Lincoln

As I came to the end of my tour of duty in the Far East I was awarded a Mentioned in Despatches for my work in the bomb dump. However, I felt a little embarrassed about this because it was really all my fellow workers and the coolies who had done the hard work. But at least it was recognition for the efforts of all the bomb dump staff in the warlike conditions and heat. I was called before the Station Commander and presented with the Oak Leaf and my GSM that had arrived by then, a very proud moment for a young country boy.

~ RAF Plumber ~

And so the end of my 2½ year tour had arrived. Before I left the island in November 1958 we had an enormous party as there were several of us travelling together back to the UK by troopship. I had been given a choice of posting in the UK and I had plumped for various stations in East Anglia in an effort to be close to home. But when the postings came through my name was down for No.16 MU RAF Stafford, a place I had never heard of.

4. Stafford

We all boarded the Troopship Empire Fowey in Singapore harbour and were allocated ship's bunks down below decks. It was quite crowded and, if I remember rightly, there were three bunks in each tier and I got the top one nearest to the pipework. We were all issued with special soap that could be used in the salt-water showers, there being no fresh water for ablutions in our part of the boat. This was going to be home for the next three weeks and in spite of the cramped conditions we just had to make the best of it.

The ship left Singapore harbour later in the day and we were all told about how life aboard would be organised. This included such things as the meal times we had been allocated, what parts of the boat were out of bounds and various regulations and safety rules that we must abide by. Next, everyone was allocated a job for the duration of the trip and I was lucky enough to be taken on as a member of the ship's entertainment team. Nothing very spectacular, all I had to do was play records and make announcements over the ship's tannoy system for one hour each lunch time. Meanwhile, my pals had got themselves taken on as Sergeants' Mess stewards, a plumb job that gave them plenty of free time and access to the special food that was usually available there.

We settled down into the pretty dull routine, I would assist my pals in the Sergeants' Mess after breakfast and do my one hour show at midday. Then I went down to the Sergeants' Mess at 1300 hours to help eat all the leftovers such as ice-cream and other treats before helping them to clear up after lunch was over. Our evenings were usually spent up on deck, it was possible to buy large jugs of beer in the canteen and we generally sat around in the balmy evenings chatting and reminiscing. Our first port of call was Colombo in Ceylon where we were all allowed ashore for a quick look around the place. I managed to take a few photographs and buy souvenirs, but generally I think we spent most of the time in a dockside bar sampling the local beer.

Troopship Empire Fowey

We set sail again, back in the shipboard routine and trying to keep cheerful. There was the occasional entertainment such as a film and of course bingo. One of the daily interests was the ship's log. There would be a sweepstake each day on the distance travelled and one could buy tickets for any mileage reckoned. We did not hear of anyone winning and suspected that it was all a fix and won by those with access to the right information. Our next stop was Aden where there had been local trouble and we were warned not to stray out of The Crater, the main area around the town. A few of us hired a taxi and were given a tour around the sights such as they were and to take a few photographs before returning to the ship.

Our trip through the Suez Canal was quite interesting; it had only just been reopened after the Suez Crisis. As we waited to pass through from Port Suez the locals tried to sell their wares and were constantly pressuring us, but I managed to keep hold of my money and was not tempted. There were many wrecked ships to view along the way and it was quite strange to be so close to the shore in places. At Port Said we were again allowed ashore for a few hours but I was not impressed and was glad to get aboard again.

An evening out on the Empire Fowey - Author right

We set off through the Mediterranean heading for Cyprus but unfortunately arrived in the dark and could only see the lights. Although we stopped out in the Bay of Limassol, it was only to pick up passengers who were brought out by a small boat. When we awoke in the morning we were on our way again and everyday heading ever further west towards Blighty. We sailed straight past the Rock of Gibraltar and were only able to take photographs from the ship, then up through the Bay of Biscay to eventually see the white cliffs of the Isle of Wight. Finally, after three weeks at sea it was up the Solent in the cold November weather with everyone on deck to get their first sight of home.

I had 60-day's leave entitlement and travelled home to Suffolk by train with my kit bags. My 'deep sea box', as it was known, followed later with all my personal possessions such as Hi Fi equipment and records and finished up at the former railway station at Capel St. Mary. From there it was brought on the railway workers trolley to the Gate House at Little Wenham. Unfortunately, we had no electricity there and I was unable to indulge in my new past time of listening to jazz on my Hi Fi kit.

But with a bit of cash in my pocket I set to and made the most of my leave. The first thing I did was get myself booked into the British School of Motoring in Ipswich for six driving lessons. I had been driving tractors at RAF Tengah and occasionally an old Hillman saloon that the Pakistani dhobi wallers across the road from the Bomb Dump owned. I had also got myself a Singapore Provisional Driving Licence so that my pal Ben was able to give me a few lessons and let me drive on the public roads. After the six lessons in Ipswich I passed the test at the first attempt and set about looking for some wheels. My boyhood pal Dobby, Robin Baldwin, sold me a little Ford 8 van. It was dark blue and black with a spare wheel on the passenger door. In the back was a seat for two, making it the ideal first vehicle for me.

During my leave I searched the map of England for Stafford and worked out my route there along the old A45 which at that time went through every town and village to the Midlands and then up the A5 to Cannock to get to Stafford. On my last day of leave I packed all my belongings into the van and late in January 1959 set off on the 185 mile journey to my new posting.

All the plumbers were billeted in Johnson Block, named after the former Battle of Britain pilot. The barrack rooms had been converted into small bunks one man to a room where I managed to squeeze in all my kit. The armament workshops were situated on No.5 Site a mile down the road and consisted of two large bays. One bay was dedicated to guns and the other to bomb carriers and their fittings. No.16 MU was a major supply depot and in the adjoining hangers were pallet upon pallet loads of guns and bomb carriers stacked up to the ceilings. An army of fork lift trucks worked all day shifting pallets around the site and providing us with a never-ending supply of work. I was assigned to work in the guns section with a Corporal Technician (Cpl/T) who was what is known as a 'squint and squeeze merchant'. In other words, his hobby was competition shooting. The guns we handled were of all calibres from .22 inches up to 20 mm canon, usually all packed in preservative grease and wrapped in protective greaseproof paper. The team in the workshop unpacked the guns and degreased them before undertaking whatever was required. Sometimes this would be pre-issue inspection, modifications, stripping for spare parts or preparation for scrap. And that was what my team was involved in. We worked outside the shed with oxyacetylene torches, cutting the guns up, or if they were large, cutting through certain sections such as the breeches, to prevent them being used again. They were then thrown on a big heap and sold off as scrap. Sometimes we would salvage certain parts that could be reused as spares or an order might come in for a rare part that we would then search out.

Twenty millimetre Hispano guns are quite heavy and we loaded rows of them on the angle-iron racks, ready for the torch. It was quite heavy work, out in the open, often in poor weather, but we tried to make it enjoyable. One scheme was a competition to see how many times you could lift one above your head, weightlifter-style. Another was to burn through the breech block area of the gun just as some dignitary was passing. Each gun was full of grease, which would come pouring out of the muzzle-end like a flame-thrower, usually causing a bit of alarm.

One day we had just finished cutting up a pallet-load of new-looking rifles that we had been told to burn. We assumed they were worn out. However, it was not long before it was found that we had been given the wrong rifles; they were all perfectly serviceable. I never did learn who got it in the neck for that one! The Cpl/T in charge of our gang was also a bit fly. He would take a spare part from here and a spare part from there, gradually squirreling away a whole gun for his collection. Whether this was official or not, I do not know, but I do recall quite a stink when the local paper published details of how the scrap dealers were able to do practically the same thing with what was supposed to be a load of scrap. From then on there were very tight controls and inspections on what we cut up and how it was disposed of, particularly handguns.

Occasionally, when we didn't have anything to cut up, we would be used on the degreasing tanks, a really filthy and unhealthy job with fumes from the chemicals. Whilst operating the cutting torches or degreasing plant my hands got really ingrained with the grease and carbon dust, so much so that I just couldn't get them clean. When back at the barrack block and preparing for a night out I resorted to using neat bleach on my hands just to get them looking presentable. Now and again we would be employed doing a bit of work on the bomb carriers, usually modifications and rewiring, etc. This was much more enjoyable and more like the engineering for which I had been trained.

Two particular incidents I remember come to mind. The degreasing tanks were not very efficient and some genius thought up a scheme to improve the process. Instead of filling the tanks with paraffin they were fitted with pipes around the inside top edges for cold water to pass through. The tanks were then filled with some substance such as CTC and the cold water pipes were supposed to prevent the liquid from evaporating. This worked quite well except that it nearly killed the operators who inhaled the fumes that escaped when anything was put in or taken out of the tanks. That idea was soon scrapped. Another incident unfortunately involved me. As at all RAF stations we were on exercise and defending our site from raiders. I was walking across the site whilst on guard and saw a workman with light bulbs and a ladder coming towards me. I asked him for his civilian identity card and, as that appeared OK, I let him go and went on my way. At the end of the exercise and the debrief it transpired that I had let an intruder into the site and what I should have noticed was that his identity card described him as having green hair. I learnt a lesson from that.

After my experiences in the Far East I was not all that keen to stay at 16 MU for too long and volunteered for another overseas posting. One usually had three choices to put down and I think I opted for Gibralter, Malta or Hong Kong. It was just a matter of sitting back and waiting for the outcome.

On the social side of things my pal Shotgun and his wife Valerie had also been posted to 16 MU and I was able to visit them often in their married quarter. But as a young single lad with transport I fell in with a bunch of other older corporals who knew their way around the place. One Scotsman in particular, another Jock Wilson, was keen on horse racing and betting and collected bets from all the lads in the workshop. He then roped me in to take the daily trip down to the bookies in Stafford to place the bets. I had become a bookies runner and although I didn't bet I was paid petrol money out of the profit and it was an opportunity to visit the pubs and cafes in the town for a 'wee half' as my friend would say. One day we went to Wolverhampton races, the first and only time I have ever been racing. While we were there we bumped into one of the corporal drivers from No.2 Motor Transport Squadron that we knew at 16 MU. We thought he was away on a trip driving his 60 foot long Queen Mary aircraft transporter somewhere in other parts of the country. He was still in his uniform and we asked how he had got to the races. It transpired that he was on his way back to 16 MU, saw that the races were on and parked his 60-foot trailer in a lay-by outside Wolverhampton. He had then driven the front tractor section to the race course car park and had a day at the races. I don't think we won very much that day but at least we had a good laugh together and I got paid my petrol money.

I found that 16 MU had a swimming team and was looking for recruits for the Maintenance Command championships that were coming up shortly. I put my name forward and went along to the training sessions, held at the swimming baths in Stafford. I had learnt to swim the breaststroke very powerfully and managed to get myself selected for the team. It was a great opportunity for a break from normal work and the team travelled down by train to RAF St Athan in Wales for the competition. We had a weekend there before the competition started and spent most of the time in the swimming pool at Barry Island or down on the beach at Llantwit Major. When the competition took place we did fairly well and earned enough points for an overall second place and a cup to take home.

I had quite a lot of contact with the local people in Staffordshire and many of the civilian workers at 16 MU came from the Potteries, where they had their own particular language. Naturally, I needed to know what they were talking about, because much of it was gobbledegook to me. The first phrase I had difficulty with was, 'Cos kick a bo agin a wo and bost ut'. Believe it or not, this translates into, 'Can you kick a ball against a wall and burst it'. One day we were in a pub and I heard a man say to a woman, 'Shust oop woot', which I found out later meant, 'Shut up woman'.

Simple really, when you know. This was just the start of my learning the local dialect.

At Oulton with Pauline October 1959

Every Tuesday night we had what is known in the RAF as a bull night, the period when everyone has to muck in and clean up the living accommodation, usually ready for inspection the next day. The personnel at 16 MU had a standing invitation to the weekly Tuesday night dances held at the GPO Training School at Yarnfield near Stone. It soon became our usual routine to get the room jobs and cleaning up done as soon as possible and then dash off to the dance via a local pub. These dances were great because there was always a live band playing and to us RAF boys, all free. It was here on 6 October 1960 that I met my future wife Pauline. We danced most of the evening and at the end of the dance had to part, I had a load of RAF lads to take back to camp in my van. We made arrangements to meet again in Stone a few days later and left it at that. Unfortunately, my new posting had come through and I was to be on my way to Malta in two weeks time.

We met as planned and had several meetings, often going out to places in the area in my van or just visiting her and her family in the village of Oulton. When it was time for me to leave we agreed to keep in touch and see how things would turn out. The main thing I had to do before going to Malta was to sell my van and with the aid of one of my betting friends was able to sell it for cash in hand to a local gypsy motor trader. At the end of October 1959 after only nine months in the UK I was off on my posting to RAF Maintenance Base Safi in Malta, a place with a lot of history to explore.

5. Safi

And so I was off to RAF Innsworth once again to go through the usual routine of preparation for an overseas tour. It was much the same process as before only this time with a different bunch of lads. For a night out I hired a car and we visited a few places around Cheltenham and Gloucester the nearest towns with a bit of life and a laugh. The flight to Malta was again in the trusty Hastings arriving at RAF Luqa later in the day. I was taken by 3-ton truck to RAF Maintenance Base Safi only about a mile from the airfield perimeter fence.

Safi had originally been an area of aircraft dispersal and emergency runway attached to RAF Luqa during WW II but was later adapted to become an independent maintenance base for the island's airfields. The old runway was no longer in use and was now fenced off and used as a gas storage compound. There was a hanger full of aircraft being stored with all the usual servicing facilities for a flying station but no runway. Instead, there was a wide road connecting Safi with Luqa and when it was time to transfer aircraft to the airfield, the road was closed and the aircraft towed to the Transit Aircraft Flight (TAF) at Luqa airfield. The living accommodation was in old wartime Nissen huts in an area close to Safi village, and although the Station Armoury had a stone built office and small arms store, the rest of the servicing facilities were also in Nissen huts. We were within easy walking distance of the village where in the popular local bar, a reused Gordon's Gin bottle filled with the village's rough wine could be bought for 1/- (5p). During the summer months, the living in personnel spent many a happy hour at Peter's Pool, a rocky bay ideal for swimming and diving; our liquid refreshment was lowered into the sea to keep it cool.

My job was servicing the aircraft in the hanger, doing repairs and modifications, and part of the team taking them to Luqa for test flights. We undertook all the normal armament operations carried out on aircraft, but we had a wide variety of aircraft to work on. There were one or two Canberra B2s, a T4 and a B(I)6, a Meteor 8, a Shackelton and often some visiting aircraft in for repair. The visitors I remember most were Canberra PR 3s from No. 39 Squadron at Luqa for modifications, a Blue Hunter of the RAF's Blue Diamonds display team that needed an engine change and a Beverley with a damaged nose. My team would remove ejection seats, guns and all the other armament fittings for servicing in the specialist bays in the Armament Section. These would then be refitted and the aircraft prepared for a test flight before either being returned to storage or given back to the original operators.

At Peter's Pool summer 1960 – Author back row second from left

For the Canberras some of the explosive devices such as canopy bolt detonators and fire extinguisher cartridges were fitted at Safi, but ejection seats were not armed, or starter cartridges fitted until we got to the TAF at Luqa. This meant a long delay at Luqa while the aircraft was armed, causing much frustration by the other ground crew members and the borrowed aircrew. To overcome this I agreed to ride inside the cockpits and arm the ejection seats whilst being towed along the road. Probably quite illegal, but one of those initiatives that sometimes saves the day. The only problem for me was the heat. Working in very cramped conditions in what is really a greenhouse in the summer months was like being in a sauna. As soon as we got to Luqa I would wring myself out and head for the nearest Coke machine for a nice cool drink.

Author arming a Meteor 8 ejection seat at RAF Luqa

Occasionally, we were allowed a ride in non-jet aircraft during the test flights and I have vivid memories of my ride in the Beverley while it was on test. About four of us persuaded the pilot that we could go on the flight and were told to ride up in the tail boom. Now the Beverley is like a great big box with wings four engines and a thick tail boom sticking out of the top rear. It is in the tail section that the paratroopers sit, and when they jump a large round hatch in the floor is opened up for them to drop through. We all climbed up into the tail boom and settled down for the flight, but unfortunately all the seats had been removed and it was just a bare shiny metal floor. But not to worry, the Beverley is a slow cumbersome old machine and we were able to stand up most of the time looking out of the small windows. We flew out over the island picking out all the landmarks and then out over the sea. This was where the pilot decided to do a thorough test of the aircraft and started to throw it around as if it were a fighter. He did sharp turns, stalls and dives all testing the capabilities of the aircraft. Up in the tail section we were sliding around on the shiny floor bumping into the sides and each other with an occasional sliding pass over the paratrooper's hatch. Thankfully the pilot then flew back and landed at Luqa with the test completed. As we climbed down and out onto terra firma we bumped into a startled looking pilot. 'Oh' he said 'I forgot you were up there, I hope you enjoyed the trip' I don't think he even knew there were no seats, and the only reason I had managed to get a ride was because I had fitted the signal pistol!

Author servicing Shackelton nose gun turret

The Safi Armament Section was also responsible for a number of other sites on the island such as Fort St. Lucien an explosives storage site at Marsaxlokk and the old airfield at Qurendi where bombs were stored out on the former runway. We also had contacts with other units such as the Fleet Air Arm airfield at Hal Far and the other RAF base at Ta'kali in the north of the island. Once a year there would be an air show at Ta'kali and we would be involved, usually with displays of equipment such as gun turrets, ejection seats and bomb carriers etc. quite a lot of effort but a nice change to the routine.

My brother Peter wrote to me to ask if I would do my best man thing at his wedding the following year. I had been writing to Pauline practically every day and she had been writing to me. This was a good opportunity to get a trip home to see her and I applied for a free indulgence flight home. The wedding would be in April and as my leave year ended on 31 March, I was able to book a few weeks leave either side of this date, using up much of my quota for the two years. I got my indulgence flight granted; this was a trip in an empty Hastings in freight fit carrying two private cars and a few seats. There were four of us as passengers and after takeoff we climbed into the cars for a very comfortable trip to the U.K. I don't suppose many people have travelled in a Hillman Minx at 10,000 feet.

I had a very enjoyable extended period of leave, hiring a car to get around and to take Pauline to meet my mother at Little Wenham. We all travelled in the hire car up to Edinburgh for the wedding that was on 16 April 1960. My mother, brother Christopher, Pauline and I all travelled together and stayed with friends and relations of Peter's new family in Scotland. After the wedding we returned via Oulton to drop Pauline off and for my mother to meet Pauline's parents. We had decided to get engaged and I did it the old fashioned way by asking permission of Pauline's father Reg to receive the family approval. A requirement of indulgence flights is that you must book a return ticket on a civilian airline to ensure that you can return to your unit. But I got a call to report to RAF Lyneham where I had been allocated a flight back to Malta, thus enabling me to cancel the airline ticket and make a good saving. This was once again on a Hastings, but just for a change we stopped at a French Naval airbase to refuel. This was a bit unusual because although we got off the aircraft and stood on the tarmac, the aircrew did the refuelling while we stood and watched.

Although I had not given Pauline an engagement ring, my first job on return to Malta was to get a ring from a local jeweller and send it off to her. There were customs restrictions at the time and in order to avoid the X-ray machines I packed it in a stainless steel tea strainer for transit through the post. I am pleased to say that it arrived safely; what became of the strainer I do not know, but Pauline still has the ring and we are still "engaged".

Back at Safi I was now saving hard because Pauline and I were planning to get married in April 1961 and an opportunity arose to earn some extra money in the year that would elapse. A British Airways Viscount aircraft had accidentally taxied into the ATC building at Luqa and was a write off. However, it was decided to salvage as much as possible and it was towed to Safi and parked. An enterprising Master Engineer in Engineering Wing got permission to take on the contract to dismantle it in off duty time. He recruited a band of us, mainly with aircraft skills, to carry out the work and pack the parts up for shipment to the U.K. For this we were paid 2/6d (12½ p) an hour tax free, but we were expected to work all weekends and evenings until the job was done.

Viscount airliner hits ATC

The engine and airframe fitters dealt with all the aircraft structure and engines whilst the rest of us dismantled the seats, fittings and anything else that didn't need too much technical know how and could be salvaged. We were on a rather tight budget and needed to scrounge packing cases and materials from anywhere we could. Being a maintenance unit there were plenty of these available but we spent a lot of our time modifying the crates to fit the parts and even removing and straightening nails for reuse. But it was a nice little earner and helped me to boost my savings quite considerably.

Salvaging the write-off Viscount

While I was at Safi I started to get myself trained up for promotion and took my Cpl/T exam, scraping through with enough scores to gain a pass. This meant I got a pay rise and turned my two chevrons upside down to denote the new rank. I was very lucky to get through that; part of the tests required me to strip and assemble a 20 mm Hispano canon a task I had only ever done once whilst in training at Halton. Under the scrutiny of the examining Flight Sergeant (Flt Sgt) I successfully remembered how to do it. However, when I got to the cartridge case extractor mechanism I forgot to fit the spring locking pin and, as I removed the part, the two springs shot out narrowly missing the examiner. I thought I had had it then, but the examiner asked me what I had done wrong, and how I would find out how to do it properly to which I gave good replies. Although I failed that element, I just scraped through with an overall pass in guns because of my good knowledge of the Hunter gun pack harmonisation, a subject I had really genned up on (studied). From that I started on the trade training and testing required for Senior Technician (Snr/T) rank.

New singles living accommodation consisting of a two-storey barrack block built of Maltese sandstone was eventually completed and we moved in, this time close to the village of Kirkop. I was allocated a nice bunk and settled down, preparing for my planned trip home to get married. The bus service to Valletta was quite regular and hire cars were easily available. There were always trips to the beach, our favourite being Peter's Pool, or to the local cinemas to keep us entertained. I got involved in the swimming team as I was a good breaststroke swimmer, having represented 16 MU in the Maintenance Command Championships. We swam in competitions against other units in the Fort St Angelo swimming lido in the Grand Harbour at Valletta and I even managed to get into the diving team as I was quite good on the springboard.

I was once again asked to be best man, this time for Ron Nicholls and Moira. He was an Engine Fitter I knew from the days when I was living in the Safi Nissen huts and she was a Wren he had met on the island. They were involved in running weekly Tombola sessions at Safi; a very popular event, attended by locals and service personnel from all over the island. The profit went into the station's Social Funds; Ron called out the numbers, Moira ran the prize draw and, once trained up, I ran the accounts book recording all the ticket sales. There were about eight of us on the team and every Wednesday and Sunday night we would have a nice little paid job to entertain us.

I booked a return airline ticket to the UK with a single one back for Pauline and left at the end of March to marry Pauline in St John's Church at Oulton in Staffordshire on 1 April 1961. If I recall I flew on a Vickers Viscount turboprop aircraft, quite a comfortable change from the Hastings that had been my main form of transport. My brother Peter was my best man and Pauline and I had a honeymoon touring the Lake District, the Isle of Skye and Scotland in a nice little Ford Popular hire car. We then flew back to Malta on another Viscount landing at Rome to refuel on the way.

I had found a nice flat at No.1b Parisio Street in Sliema and we settled down to married life and the second half of my Malta tour. I managed to buy a Vespa scooter and we were now able to travel around easily and I had independent transport to get to work at Safi. The hours of work were 0700 to 1300 hours six days a week, a nice arrangement that left every afternoon free for the beach or shopping etc. Every day I had to pass the main entrance of RAF Luqa on the way to work.

1b Parisio Street, Sleima

One day I was pulled in by a RAF policeman who charged me with not wearing my beret. It transpired that one either had to wear a crash helmet or a beret when riding a motorcycle. I protested that I could not wear a beret on a scooter and it was not law to wear a crash helmet at that time in Malta. This was the one and only time I had to face a disciplinary charge during thirty years service and luckily for me when the charge came up before my CO, I merely received an admonishment, on the understanding that I would purchase a crash helmet.

There was plenty to do in my off duty time, I continued with the twice weekly Tombola work and Pauline joined Moira to help run the raffle. At other times Pauline and I travelled around to all the places of interest. We visited Mosta Dome, the fourth-largest unsupported dome in Europe, the pre historic catacombs, the ancient city of Medina, the old buildings of Valletta, including the infamous 'Gut' or Straight Street as it is properly called. Then there were trips to Gozo Island on the local ferry and for one day we hired a local fisherman and his boat to take a party of us out to Comino, a lovely uninhabited island between Gozo and Malta. We took plenty of refreshment with us as you can imagine, but the sea got a little choppy, the sun was very hot and one or two in the party started to feel a little seasick. But we had a good day out and had visited somewhere that normally we would not have done and was not available by public transport.

A day out to Comino – Author with hat, Pauline behind

One day Pauline and I were walking along the main street in Valetta and a local came up to me and started to talk to me in Maltese, a very difficult language. Once he realised I was not Maltese he apologised and asked us in English what he wanted to know. It seems that I had got such a good tan and with black hair he had identified me as Maltese. On another occasion we were walking along the sea front in Sliema and a matelot in square rig uniform came the other way who seemed to recognise me. We both stopped and eyed each other up and said practically simultaneously 'I know you from somewhere don't I?' Well we went through our life histories and all the places we had been posted and eventually agreed that we didn't know each other and parted. It was just one of those things that happen when you have met so many people and been to so many places.

Pauline inspecting a Canberra PR3

We visited and swam in all the numerous beaches and coves around the island, particularly Peter's Pool, where most of the plumbers usually congregated. In the nice warm sea I managed to teach Pauline to swim, a feat I was able to repeat with both my daughters in later years. I was once again roped in for the swimming competitions; this time for an official Station Swimming Gala that would be contested between the single lads who lived on camp and the married men who lived off-base. I volunteered to captain the married men's team and a lad called Paddy McGoran captained the singles team. We set about recruiting our swimmers, secretly carrying out trials to find the fastest in each stroke and the best divers. Unfortunately, we both found that no one could do the butterfly stroke and, as this was one of the events, we considered dropping it from the schedule. But my habit of volunteering overcame me and I suggested that we keep the event and both go away and learn how to do it. I set about practising this very tiring stroke and luckily my breaststroke ability made it a bit easier. But I never did learn the proper dolphin kick, just managing to do a normal breaststroke kick to keep me going. On the day of the event I had no idea how Paddy had got on with his training, only that like me he had achieved something that looked like the butterfly. There were one or two others game to have a go, but the main competition was from Paddy. It was only one 50-metre length of the lido and off we went with much splashing and no idea where the rest of them were. At the end and after swallowing a few mouthfuls of water I touched the end exhausted but triumphant as I had won quite easily. Paddy came in second and told me that he knew I would win as he had a married friend who had been watching me practice. The married boys won the cup and as usual we all had a good party afterwards to celebrate.

I had been lucky to have half of my Malta tour as a single person and half married, the best of both worlds. As I was now married I needed to extend my tour to the full three years that married men usually undertook. To do this it was necessary for me to apply to higher authority and as there was no pre-printed form for this the RAF required a General Application Form (Gen App) to be completed. This really was a letter with rather old-fashioned wording as follows:

To the Commanding Officer, RAF Maintenance Base, Safi.

Sir,
I 588577 Cpl Anderton M have the honour to request that I be granted permission to extend my overseas tour in Malta from 2½ years to 3 years on the grounds that I am now married.
I remain Sir,
Your obedient Servant,
Cpl M Anderton.

Thankfully I received the necessary permission. I understand that the Gen App, as it is known, is still in use in the RAF today.

Summer and winter uniforms

Our social life was quite hectic, we had no children and were therefore able to attend all the numerous parties, outings and events that took place within our sphere of friends. We became particularly friendly with another armourer, Bill Paice and his wife Pat, often at the beach together or just sitting at the local bar until quite late chatting and joking. Bill had bought himself a little 1953 Morris Minor car quite cheaply and decided to overhaul it and get it back to the UK when the time came to leave. As we would be leaving at the same time, Pauline and I agreed to assist with the venture and started the plans to drive it back overland. But first we had to have the engine out for an overhaul, including a regrind of the crankshaft. It was quite a long hot sweaty job, but we got it all back together and running quite well. The interior of the car was refurbished by a local body repair shop in pale blue to match the exterior at a price of £9.

It was time once again to apply for a choice of posting on our pending return to the UK and naturally I opted for Stafford so that Pauline could be close to home. She had never been out of the country before and it was quite a shock to her system to be away in a foreign land for 18 months with no physical contact with home. The closest to that was when my mother and brother Christopher came to stay with us for two weeks holiday as also did her friend Kathleen Bolton. A lad she new called Graham Bunn from Moddershall and later Jimmy Moulson from Stone, who were both in the Navy, were also able to visit us to have a good chat about home and Staffordshire.

When the posting came through it was to No.5131 Bomb Disposal Squadron RAF Stafford a pleasant surprise, only six miles from Pauline's home. Bill and I got the car overhaul finished and booked tickets for ourselves, wives and the car on the Italian ferry that plied between Malta and Sicily. It was our plan to drive up the leg of Italy, camping whenever we could or until it got too cold, generally making a holiday of our return trip home to the UK. Once we had got all our possessions boxed up and into stores for transport by the RAF, and the flats where we lived handed back to the Maltese owners, we left the island.

6. Eight Days from Malta

The following chapter was written in 1962 just after we had got back to the UK and while it was still fresh in my memory. I had hoped that it would be published one day and, although I sent a copy off to the Readers Digest, nothing came of it. Apart from some editing to avoid repetition and to correct the spelling and grammar, this is what I wrote: -

In order that we had no time limits, the only part of our journey that was prearranged was the passage to Sicily, which, because the fares go up out of season, was the most expensive time. On payment of £35 we had tickets on the ss. Citta de Tunis sailing on October 6th 1962. For the journey we limited each person, to one suitcase, plus one small travel bag per couple; that was the roof rack loaded. We also decided that we would camp where possible and cook meals at the roadside to cut expenses a little and that filled the boot.

Aboard the SS Citta de Tunis   *A brew up at the roadside*

Bill's 1953 Morris Minor, roof rack covered with a shower curtain, four adults and a boot full of camping gear looked like a covered wagon heading west. At noon on the 6th with the car loaded aboard, we set sail under the Italian flag for Syracuse. Bill and I agreed not to shave and had got two days growth on our departure; to the passengers we probably looked like crew. Not speaking Italian, our first problem was the Sicilian Customs Officer who spoke no English. For awhile we listened to him putting over what he wanted but it was no use, he couldn't even speak in hand signs. At last a little man who spoke English arrived and told us that two suitcases were required for inspection. This had us worried, Bill and I had bought 1,000 cigarettes each before leaving and we couldn't remember which cases they were in. Just in time the answer came, Bill took his case and I took Pat's, the officer thought there were 1,000 cigarettes between four of us. We tipped our translator ten cigarettes and set off in the dark streets of Syracuse for Messina and the ferry to the mainland.

Shouts and flashing lights soon brought home the fact that we were in a one-way street going in the wrong direction. But we pressed on through the town and into the Sicilian night with thoughts of the Mafia and Mount Etna as we went. Our first stop for petrol turned out to be a fiasco. With our lack of Italian, we were baffled for awhile but realised that the easiest way was writing the amount required in litres in the dust on the boot.

At 2315 hours we reached Messina and found it deserted with no sign of the ferry. A small boy wandered along the street and using guidebook Italian and pigeon English, directed us to the midnight ferry. He left with five cigarettes in his pocket and for 30/- (£1.50) we had tickets for the European mainland - Italy's 'Big Toe'. An hour later we drove off at Villa San Giovani and travelled north until 0200 hours where we pulled off the road; it wasn't long before everyone was asleep, too tired to bother with the tent. Before it was light we were awakened by a strange noise, wondering what was happening we sat tight, listening and waiting. As dawn came we realised the locals were off to the fields, the potato harvest was in full swing.

When everyone was awake and it was light, we drove north until we found a beautiful glade bathed in sun at the roadside, an ideal place to camp. On went the Primus stoves for hot water and after a wash and a cup of tea we all felt a lot livelier and prepared our breakfast. It was wonderful after a long night drive, lounging under the trees in the sun, relaxed and refreshed we felt on top of the world.

Breakfast in the shade

Nightfall brought us to Scalea on Italy's 'ankle' where we made our first night camp. After driving around corners all day we were tired and pitched the tent on a small hill off the road and had tinned steak and kidney pie before preparing for bed. The ex-Army tent was just big enough for our four airbeds which, after Malta's beaches, were not in mint condition. The girls put on night clothes, as if they were still at home, but Bill and I just took off our shoes and got our heads down, occupying the two outer positions with the girls in the middle. With one blanket between two we were soon all asleep. An hour later I awoke touching down on terra firma. "This is going to be an uncomfortable night" I thought, every hour I would have to blow up my airbed if I wanted any sleep. After two hours I pushed Pauline over on her bed and got to sleep again, a little squashed but comfortable.

The next morning we awoke to find it chilly and I was glad I had kept my clothes on as this enabled me to get the stoves on straight away. It was another fine day and we all tucked in to a hearty breakfast. After striking camp we were off along the winding coast road hoping to make Naples before nightfall. Going up the long ascent to Monto Antillo our overloaded car decided to rest and spluttered to a halt. With luck we found the contact breakers needed cleaning and it wasn't long before we were at the top. The scenery was very picturesque with chestnut trees alongside the road, where we gathered up nuts like squirrels. An old Italian soon appeared and talked to us in English. He then disappeared into the woods before returning with a large bag of nuts for us. With gratitude we offered him cigarettes, but to our amazement he pulled out a packet of English cigarettes; his son, he said, was a seaman and sent home cigarettes every week. We said goodbye and pressed on for Naples.

It was quite a change when we reached the Autostrada at Salerno; for 3/6d (17½p) we had the facilities of a motorway, wonderful service stations, restaurants and charming scenery. With our overloaded carriage we managed 50mph and apart from more misfiring had a smooth run into Naples, in pouring rain, just after nightfall. This meant no camping, but we soon found a hotel and booked two rooms, one with a bath, only to find there was no hot water. But after a cold bath we felt like human beings again and decided to have a look around and sample the Italian beer. It tasted rather watery, but after a couple we found it was really quite good.

After a good night's sleep we went south again to Pompeii and for 2½ hours wandered around, marvelling at the ruins and feeling disappointed at the state of repair and shoulder-high weeds. Wondering what the Government was doing with the entrance fees, we returned to the car and reloaded the roof-rack (every time we parked we had to lock everything inside). Hoping to make Rome that day, we found the Naples-to-Rome Autostrada very pleasant, gliding through the countryside, passing Monte Cassino, through the mountains and over the valleys. On striking the Rome ring-road, we made for a campsite near Lido de Roma.

It was a wonderful camping ground, a slope dotted with pine trees, leaving a carpet of needles, a shop, restaurant, showers and even razor points with 110- and 220-volt sockets. Pitching our scruffy tent near an American canvas 'house' we cooked and ate our meal, after which, with the scent of pine, we sat round talking of the trip and counting the cash! Tomorrow we would look around Rome and try to make Pisa in the afternoon.

With the fourth night over, we drove to Rome, parked in a side street and walked to the Coliseum, then on to Saint Peter's Square, passing the National Monument. Nearing the square, priests and religious shops became more frequent and after taking photographs, we started back for the car. The horse-drawn taxis seemed very expensive so we took a motor taxi instead. We were soon speeding through the traffic, disappointed at not having time to have a good look around the beautiful city.

Out in the country again we stopped to cook our midday meal, fresh milk and bread having been purchased in Rome. Motoring on, we by-passed Livorno at dusk and arrived in Pisa at a time when the streets were quiet. Due to its northerly position the temperature was unsuitable for camping and after a tour round we found a riverside hotel for the night. A highlight of our stay here was the highly decorated toilet pan, covered inside and out with flowers. It fascinated us so much that I took a photograph. I don't know what the other guests thought on seeing a man taking a camera and flashgun in with him!

In the morning we had a look at the tower-on-the-tilt, a chat with some English tourists and a good stretch of the legs. Pleased at having seen the tower we drove out of Pisa and joined the Autostrada again, this time for a long haul to Milan. At Florence we joined the famous 'Highway of the Sun', viaducts, tunnels, wonderful service and eating areas and fast motoring for miles. Our meals in the bridge-type restaurants were superb after camp cooking. Pauline and I still refer to two pieces of bacon and an egg as 'bacon and egg a la Autostrada'.

Taking turns at the wheel we finally arrived in Milan, a bustling city and very confusing for strangers, but somehow we found a hotel on the outskirts and got in another good night's sleep.

Decorated hotel toilet at Pisa

Finding we were opposite the local market Pauline and Pat went shopping while Bill and I did a quick service on the car. They came back loaded with goodies, including a kilo of Italian tomatoes that we fried up together with bacon and sausage for our breakfast as soon as we were clear of the city. Sipping coffee in the sun, we watched the traffic and wondered how we would fare in the mountains ahead. Passing through Northern Italy ever upward to the Simplon Pass, the lakeside road through Stresa, was charming, reminding us of Britain's Lakeland.

Getting quickly through the Swiss Customs, we were soon in mountainous country and saw the heights ahead. Going up the steep roads the car decided to rest and for a few moments we took in the scenery and air while Bill fixed the engine. It struggled to the top of Simplon, through tunnels and past snow patches. Thankful that we had beaten the winter snow, we started the long descent into Switzerland heading for Lausanne that night and making good progress along the Rhone valley, stopping at Montreux for coffee and to cash traveller's cheques with the cafe proprietor.

A quick service before the mountains

In Lausanne the problem was finding accommodation for the night, after an hour searching we gave up and went to the local police station where the Gendarme, after a few telephone calls, found a hotel for us. The next morning in the town we found the prices very high and made the most of buying a few souvenirs and decided to drive on and see what France was like, leaving Lausanne at 1300 hours.

The French restaurants and cafes were also expensive and we thought the best plan was an all night drive to Calais. Passing Rheims at 2200 hours the roads and weather were ideal for driving, but the front passenger had to stay awake to navigate and chat to the driver to keep him awake while the other pair were asleep in the back. At 0400 hours we hit fog 20 miles from Calais and pulled off the road to sleep and wait for daybreak. Before dawn we were awakened by a crash and a curse from outside, seconds later a face peered through the window shouting in French; sleepily we tried to discover what was going on. Pat and I knew a little French and realised that we had parked on the cycle track and a workman had run into us because we had no lights.

We waited for dawn before driving on and found that the fog got thinner on approaching Calais. Touring the town at 0700 hours we found a cafe and ordered tea. The cafe proprietor didn't leave us enough milk and I went to the kitchen door for some more, as I opened it an Alsatian dog went for my arm missing by a hair. I quickly retreated without the milk, we had come this far and wanted to make it all the way.

Arrival at Dover

The car ferry left at 1100 hours and we had plenty of time for a wash and sort out of the equipment before boarding. We were feeling quite pleased with ourselves having crossed France in 18 hours, we were really on the last leg. After Customs clearance and a meal in Dover we headed for Dartford where Bill and Pat said goodbye, the end of our fascinating 1,200 miles in eight days and the start of five weeks leave.

7. Bomb Disposal

We now had the problem of travelling back to Pauline's home in Staffordshire and decided to stay the night in Kent before travelling the next day. After roughing it for eight days we found a lovely old coaching inn, booked a room and made ourselves comfortable. It was great to be back, sampling the comforts, sights, sounds and smells of England. The next day we hired a nice smart modern Ford Anglia from a nationwide hire company, loaded all our kit in and set off home for a few week's leave and to meet all the family again.

We managed to return the hire car to the local branch and made arrangements to buy our first car. We went to the showrooms at Tean and bought a nice little nearly new Ford Escort. This was the original version, an estate model of the box shape Ford Popular. It was pale green, van shaped with sliding side windows, a fold down rear seat, 1175cc side valve engine and a three-speed gearbox. As we drove away from the showroom we had a little incident while overtaking a bus. As I changed gear the gear knob came off in my hand and I missed the gear. But we pulled back in safely and eventually came to love our little car.

On my first day back off leave in January 1963 I reported to the Headquarters of No.5131 Bomb Disposal (BD) Squadron thinking this would be the start of a daily commute to work. But I was mistaken, the squadron had operational flights working in various parts of the UK and I was to be attached to No.6235 BD Flight based at RAF Acklington in Northumberland. This flight was responsible for BD operations north of the Humber and was currently working on the old bombing and gunnery range at Druridge Bay.

I had a week of initial training learning how to use mine locators, pumps and other bits of equipment at the HQ at 16 MU. Before I made my way up to Acklington I was issued with items of special clothing including wellington boots and a big thick sweater, it was clearly going to be a cold wet job. So I set out for the unknown north, leaving Pauline at home with her parents. Our plan was for me to travel home at weekends and for her to get a job locally until we found somewhere to live.

RAF Acklington was a Flying Training School with Jet Provosts buzzing round all the time. No.6235 BD Flight had around twenty men and a base in a hut on the edge of the airfield. There was a Flight Lieutenant and a Flight Sergeant in charge, a couple of other SNCOs and the rest other ranks, a mix of Scots, Geordies, Yorkshire lads and one or two southerners like me. On my first day I sat down in the Airmen's Mess for the evening meal at a large table with a gang of these lads all very cheerful and welcoming. A big Glaswegian sitting next to me elbowed me in the ribs and said 'Twa slice o' breed'. I had no idea what he was talking about, until someone explained that he wanted me to pass him two slices of bread. I soon got to grips with the northern lingo; they were just a great bunch of rough and ready chaps who got on with the job in hand.

Everyday we went out on a 3-ton truck to the Druridge Bay Range, now disused and being prepared to be handed back to the farmers. Our task was to scour every inch of it with mine locators to verify that there were no unexploded items around and to certify it safe. The area was marked out acre by acre with white tapes about two yards apart and we would spend all day going up and down the lines checking for metallic objects with mine locators and digging up anything we found. There would be one man on the locator and one man behind with a spade and a sandbag to carry the thousands of shell cases that we found. Several pairs operated at a time and the sections were quickly cleared before moving on to the next patch.

We used standard lightweight Mk 4C transistorised bomb locators, but there were also one or two of the older Mk 4A valve versions that were quite heavy and had to be carried in a backpack. Although we all had a go at every aspect of the job, I was generally teamed up with another corporal, Dave Blyth, to move all the white tapes onto a new patch that we had measured out ready for clearance. Dave was a very interesting chap that I was to meet several times in my service. He had been a young recruit in the

Army in WWII and been captured by the Japanese at the fall of Singapore. He survived that and on his return home had signed up in the RAF as a plumber.

Wet feet at Druridge Bay – Author left

To clear areas of water such as ponds we had to pump out the contents before wading in with the mine locators. When there was a pond to clear in the patch we were working on, everyone wanted to have a go in order to break up the routine a little. And this sometimes caused a few problems. First we had to get the pumps going, if it was fairly shallow we could manage with simple lightweight rotary pumps that need priming with water before they would suck. If it were a big pond, we would bring in the Coventry Climax Fire Pump with its high pressure operation and much greater capacity. If there were a lot of mud and sludge we had a Millers Pump, a machine with a bellows like chamber and a heavy clack valve that slammed shut on each downward stroke. Then it was into the pond with waders and mine locators, taking care not to sink right in. Luckily, the Air Sea Rescue helicopter from Acklington was often around and on the odd occasion was called in to pull someone free. This often led to their waders being left behind in the pond: there are probably several pairs still there today.

After a couple of months I was sent on a Bomb Disposal course at the Royal Engineers' Bomb Disposal School at Horsham in West Sussex. This was an intensive four-week course covering many aspects of the job, much of which had been practised during WWII. But there were new pieces of equipment and techniques being introduced such as shaped charges and how to deal with postwar aircraft weapons. But it was all very interesting, not just learning the history of the work but also the in depth theory of explosives, and practical work using the real thing on the range down at Lydd Marshes. At the end of the course I was a qualified Bomb Disposal Operative and entitled to wear the Bomb Disposal Badge. All I needed now was practical experience.

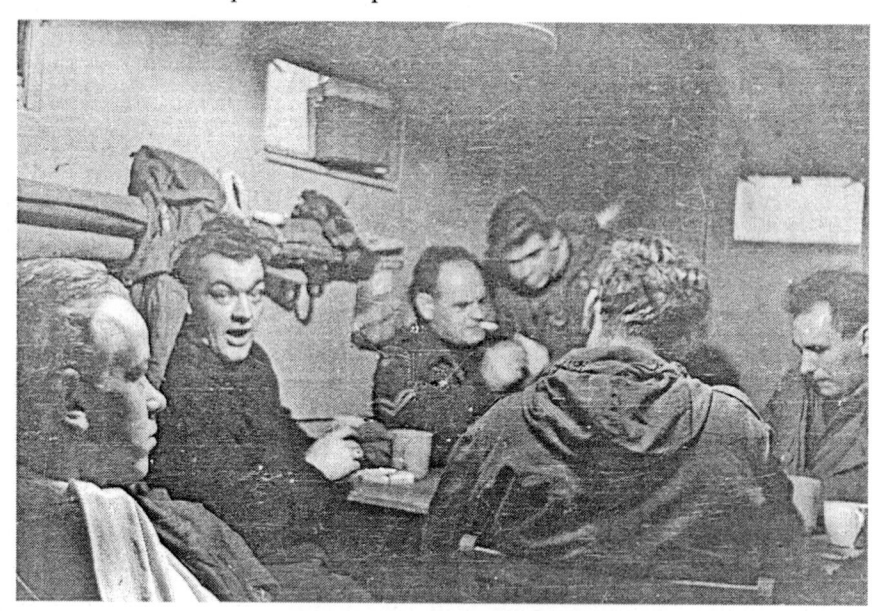

Winter tea break at Druridge Bay

Back up at Acklington the SNCOs were responsible for BD call outs to all points north and often went to check out reports of devices that had been reported to the police. Us poor 'erks' just got on with the clearance work, a healthy outdoor life that produced many characters. At lunch times we all stopped and sat in the caravan like vehicles we had for a crewroom. Our meals were brought out in heated containers, tea was brewed on site and we all stuffed our faces before having a quick game of cards, a smoke or whatever you fancied doing according to the weather. At the end of the day we all packed up the kit and were transported in the 3-ton truck back to Acklington, for tea and free time relaxation.

Naturally we usually headed for the NAAFI or the local pub, I believe it was at the Station Arms in Acklington village, where I remember some local character often brought his horse into the bar for a pint. At other times we would all head off to one of the Working Men's Clubs in the area where we were allowed in after showing our Form 1250 identity card. These places were great because there was always entertainment on, the beer was very cheap and we got to know the locals. We were allowed to use the 3-ton truck for recreational runs in the evenings and it often fell to me to be in charge of the party, although our Flight MT driver would be behind the wheel. Everything was fine until it was time to go back to camp. With a party of heavy drinking northerners all milling around it was a tough job getting them back on the truck. But I resolved the problem by getting on first and telling the driver to start the engine, they knew then that if we went without them it was a very long walk back. It seemed to work and there was never any problem again.

At weekends as soon as we were released on a Friday evening after work I would head off in my car to get home to Pauline. She had got a job as an assistant cook in Stone and although she had to work on Saturdays, I was able to transport her there and back. Sometimes I would have a passenger on the trip home from Acklington, one of the lads who lived en route and would pay for his ride with some cash for my petrol. After a weekend in the Stone area I would leave again on Sunday evening and drive all the way back up to Acklington. This was a bit hairy at times especially when the weather was bad, one night in the fog I accidentally drove the wrong way up a dual carriageway section of the A1 that was under construction.

The car performed quite well within the limits of its specification, but after a bit I found I was losing water and noted that the cylinder head gasket had blown. I took some leave and Pauline persuaded a family friend to allow me to use their garage for a few days. I removed the cylinder head and had it skimmed flat to cure the cause of the problem, reassembled the whole thing and readjusted the valves. Quite an easy job on a side valve engine. Back on the road and into the routine of long weekend use I found that there were deposits building up on the spark plug electrodes that made it difficult to start unless first cleaned. A chat with an expert on these matters revealed that I needed a cooler grade of spark plug and, after changing them over, found that everything was fine again.

After a few months the work at Druridge Bay was completed and the BD Flight moved en masse to Scotland. We were to be based at RAF Leuchars and our work commitment was to clear Tentsmuir range in the forest and sand dunes to the north. The office, stores and main equipment servicing staff were based at RAF Turnhouse just outside Edinburgh. On arrival at Leuchars we were allocated a room in a barrack block and life continued in a similar pattern, clearing large areas of land with mine locators ready to be handed back for civilian use. Most of the range was set on the edge of the conifer woods and stretched down to a sandy beach. There were salmon traps on the shoreline and on very hot days we even managed to have a dip in the sea.

I continued to drive up and down the country at weekends, quite a tiring affair in a small car. It meant that on many a day after work and a meal I would collapse on my bed and fall asleep, not waking until the next morning and just in time for breakfast. But it kept me out of mischief and saved my money. Otherwise it was out with the lads learning all about 'a pint of heavy', 'a wee half' and 'a mealy pudding'. One day the flight sergeant asked if I would like to work at Turnhouse as NCO i/c equipment, a full time job servicing all the various items of BD equipment that were held by the flight to enable all types of BD work to be undertaken. Naturally I jumped at the chance, and moved my kit and myself to a barrack block on the station.

This seemed to be a bit more settled and Pauline and I decided that she should move up to Edinburgh so that we could live together. I found a bedsit in Grange Loan and brought Pauline up in June 1963. I was able to drive to work everyday while in her spare time, Pauline was able to explore Edinburgh or visit my brother Peter's in-laws who lived in the city.

Summer tea break on the Tentsmuir Range

I was now part of the Management and occasionally got to go on the call outs when members of the public had found something they thought was explosive. We had one call to visit a RAF Marine Craft unit up the East Coast because they had picked up some dud flares, a nice ride out with one of the SNCOs into the countryside for the day.

But one of the other call outs was not quite so pleasant. There had been a call to the police from a shepherd at Inverrary on the West Coast to say that he had found an unexploded bomb up in the mountains. My Flt Sgt Jack Hatton and I drove across to Inverrary in a RAF staff car with a few bits of kit to deal with the device. On the way he complained of indigestion and we stopped to buy some Rennies. At Inverrary the shepherd led us up into the mountains, it was about six miles to the spot we were looking for. As I neared the device, poor old Jack dropped to the ground a few yards behind me. I thought he was just exhausted, but he had collapsed and died.

We were now in a bit of a fix as to what to do. I decided to send the shepherd back to call for help while I waited with the body for the help to arrive. After about four hours an Air Sea Rescue helicopter came over and the pilot landed nearby. A member of the crew checked the body before loading us aboard. The shepherd was also aboard to show them where I was and we took off for Inverrary. The pilot landed at Inverrary Castle where we dropped the shepherd off and gave statements to the waiting police. The next problem I had was the RAF staff car. Although I had a civilian driving licence, this was a RAF vehicle for which a RAF licence was officially required. Another problem was that the body could not be taken out of the District until it had been cleared by the local Coroner. After a delay of about an hour it was all fixed up. While we were on the ground the pilot had been able to phone back to Turnhouse to advise them of the situation and obtained permission for me to drive the vehicle back. When permission came from the Coroner, the pilot was able to take off to transport the body back to Turnhouse. I drove back alone and returned the vehicle to the MT Section before being debriefed by my CO. I got home very late that night, the end of a very long and traumatic day. And the bomb? It turned out to be a brass and copper rain gauge with a description of what it was engraved around the rim, placed there by some university research team.

By September 1963 the work at Tentsmuir range was finished and the BD Flight moved to RAF Topcliffe in Yorkshire, a flying training unit with Varsity aircraft near Thirsk. Because we were also moving the Flight HQ to Topcliffe, Pauline moved back to Stone temporarily while I organised my part of the Flight's move. All the equipment was loaded aboard 3-ton trucks and we set out in convoy style to our new base in North Yorkshire.

The new task was to clear the bomb dump areas of several former airfields to the east of York before they were handed back for civilian use. Once everyone was settled in, work began again and the clearance routine continued. However, the type of terrain was much different here, with wooded embankments, old buildings and bomb storage areas to deal with. This meant we would be using a lot of new equipment to cut around trees, clear undergrowth and pump out ponds.

I had a few weeks living in the barrack block with the lads at Topcliffe and was quite lucky to see Buddy Rich and his band in the NAAFI during this time. But I was soon able to find somewhere for Pauline and I to live. In the charming little village of Hutton Sessay we rented two rooms with a shared bathroom in a farmhouse called Mount Pleasant, the farmer and his family taking up the rest of the house. Thrown in was the use of half of a double garage, all a few miles from Topcliffe. Once Pauline had moved in she decided to work in the local chicken packing factory at Dalton, and we settled down again to a tranquil village life.

Meanwhile after a month or so, it was realised that the sites we would be working on were quite remote from Topcliffe and a lot of equipment was required for use each day. It was decided that we would set up a field kitchen at each site we worked on and our resident Leading Aircraftsman (LAC) cook would cook a midday meal out there for all the crew. Also, because the equipment needed regular attention I would operate at the working site, managing the equipment and assisting the cook.

Clearing RAF Elvington – Author centre front

At the start of each day we would assemble at Topcliffe, the cook and I would collect rations for all the living-in personnel and we would set out on a Bedford coach for the work site. The married men who wanted a meal would pay the equivalent of their ration money into a kitty and on the way we would stop at a local shop and buy extra rations so that we could provide a meal for everyone. We were usually able to get enough from the Airmen's Mess to feed everyone which meant that with the cash we were able to buy a few luxuries such as the occasional ice-cream, fish and chips on Fridays or sometimes a bottle of beer for everyone.

We managed to build a portable timber-framed and corrugated sheet shed to cook in; three sides and a roof with a large panel front that hinged up to double as a roof over the serving area and as a lockable door at night. To cook we had double burner petrol pressure stoves and a Hydraburner, a large pressurised petrol flamethrower style machine that could boil a gallon of water in a few minutes. The LAC cook and I had such a slick operation going that we were able to serve omelette or bacon sandwiches halfway through the morning with tea and coffee and often something during the afternoon tea break.

By this time I had a RAF licence to drive the 3-ton truck and water bowser trailer, one of my jobs was to find a local source of clean water and keep the bowser topped up with drinking water. There was always fuel required for the equipment we were using including an Allen Scythe, various pumps and a forerunner of what is now called a brushcutter. It was a bit heavy to wield around and had a lethal blade on the end of the shaft that consisted of four triangular agricultural mower blades bolted to a rotating disc. This head could also be removed and a chainsaw head fitted for clearing small trees and bushes, a useful tool, as many of the old bomb dumps were overgrown with rhododendrons and small trees. Everything had to be cleared in order to get the bomb locators through.

We had some interesting finds on these sites, plenty of buried ammunition, explosive devices and other equipment that had been disposed of by burying during WWII. On one occasion I was pumping out a small pond with the Millers Pump when I noticed that the clack valve was not operating properly. On investigation I found that some small objects were being sucked up and preventing the valve from slamming shut. I closed the machine down only to find that these objects were sensitive bomb detonators that had been thrown in the pond at some time and I was the one who had found them. Needless to say we cleared the pond by other means and eventually salvaged a whole sandbag full of detonators.

While we were at Topcliffe a job came up for us in the Isle of Man that required a party to work there for a few months. A SNCO, two corporals and a gang of about six volunteers travelled on the ferry with their equipment to do the job on the old airfield at RAF Jurby. They stayed in bed-and-breakfast accommodation in Ramsey, a rare change from the Airmen's Mess and barrack block living. The corporals were rotated every two weeks and my time came to travel over on the ferry to do my stint. It was a nice break from the routine and more like a holiday as we were able to visit most of the tourist attractions during our time off.

In my spare time at Mount Pleasant I bought a second hand Lambretta scooter and set about refurbishing it in the garage. With Pauline working we also decided to buy a new car and ordered a Vauxhall Viva from the local dealer in Thirsk. In order to save money I was able to collect it from the factory at Luton, travelling down by train using one of my free railway warrants. Whilst buying spares for the scooter in York I found they had several scooters for sale very cheap because they had major faults such as crankshaft damage etc. This was the start of a nice little earner. As I sold one machine I would buy in another for about £5 and go through the operation to repair and refurbish it. Unfortunately, my insurance company eventually stopped me, as they would not insure me for commercial operations.

Two notable events in the history of the RAF occurred while I was at Topcliffe, the first was the updating of the personal service numbering system that had been in operation for many years. I had two letters added to my number and was issued with a computer readable card that showed that my new number was to be J0588577. The second event occurred in 1964 when the Armed Forces Pay Review Board agreed the proposed new trade structure arrangements. This event was much more drastic and concerned the long awaited changes to pay and rank. Every trade and rank in the RAF had been evaluated according to a scale of benefit to the work of the service and we all gathered to hear the results. On the appointed day Armament Fitters would become Aircraft Technician Weapons (A.Tech(W)) and would be in the top band of the pay structure, recognising the technicalities of working on aircraft. As a result the Corporal Technician rank was abolished and I reverted to plain Corporal with my stripes up the right way again but with a substantial pay rise.

Pauline and I had decided to apply for another overseas posting and this time we were selected for Germany with a posting to RAF Wildenrath. Just before the time came to leave Topcliffe I was presented with an Air Officer Commanding-in-Chief's (AOC) Commendation for my 3-years work on the BD Flight, a time when I had made a lot of new friends and gained a whole new batch of experiences. When we left Yorkshire in December 1965 Pauline moved back to Stone to stay with her parents and after Christmas I drove the Viva to Germany via Dover and Ostend.

8. Wildenrath

Early in January 1966 I travelled to Germany with all my kit packed in the Viva. It was not the first time I had driven on the right of the road but it was a bit nerve racking, especially navigating on my own through the centre of Brussels. But I made it to RAF Wildenrath where I moved into the barrack block and soon started my arrival procedure.

At the Armament Squadron I met up with the other plumbers and one of these happened to be Al Wilson a J/T I had worked with on Bomb Disposal. He had a flat in the village of Wassenberg nearby and invited me for a meal and to meet his wife Kay. Their flat was in the basement of a four storey house and they told me that there was an empty flat available on the very top floor. The German owner, who also lived in the house, showed me around and I immediately paid a month's rent in advance.

Al Wilson and Author (right) at RAF Wildenrath

The next thing was to organise getting Pauline out from the UK. I found that there were regular civilian charter flights from Gatwick to Wildenrath organised by the RAF for families, friends and personnel travelling on leave. As soon as I could, I booked a flight for her and she travelled on 28 January 1966, less than a month after I had arrived.

At that time RAF Wildenrath was home to two Squadrons of Canberras, No.14 Squadron had B(I)8s and a T4 and No.17 Squadron had PR7s and a T4. The RAF Germany Communications Squadron was also based there and flew Pembrokes, Doves and a Heron.

The station was continually prepared for a Warsaw Pact invasion of West Germany during the Cold War and our B(I)8s could carry a variety of armament such as a gun pack with four 20 mm Hispano canons, conventional bombs and nuclear bombs. They could also perform the LABS (Low Altitude Bombing System) technique that released a bomb in an upward climb, allowing ballistics to deliver the weapon while the aircraft turned for home. But the greatest effort was put into the nuclear role, using an American bomb that was stored, serviced, and delivered to the aircraft by American personnel. There were permanently two B(I)8s loaded with live nuclear weapons on permanent standby in a locked and guarded compound known as QRA (Quick Reaction Alert). There was also living accommodation in the compound to house two complete aircrews and the associated ground crew who were locked inside the wire 24 hours a day to react instantly when required.

I was assigned to the Ejection Seat bay in the Armament Squadron HQ building, working with other corporals and J/Ts for Sgt Bob Ashley the NCO i/c. I was now involved in very technical work once again, requiring the very highest standard of workmanship at all times. The plumbers on the squadrons or from ASF would disarm and remove the ejection seats from the aircraft for servicing every six months and bring them to us for inspection. This entailed stripping the components from each seat and taking certain parts such as safety equipment, and oxygen systems to other sections for inspection. The rest of the seat structure was completely dismantled, cleaned, inspected, tested, lubricated, modified and finally reassembled. Some of the clockwork mechanisms received particular attention such as timing tests before being refitted to the seat. One exciting part of the work was to meet the aircrew after they had used an ejection seat. They were so grateful that we had played a part in saving their lives in an emergency situation, we would often get a crate of beer as a thank you gift, an informal tradition in the RAF.

As most plumbers will know, when on an active station, there are always secondary tasks to be performed in time of war, alerts or exercise etc. At Wildenrath most of Armament Squadron plumbers became involved with the 14 Sqdn plumbers in loading nuclear weapons to the B(I)8 Canberras and we were formed into permanent loading teams of four men and an NCO i/c. But because the weapons belonged to the Americans there was a very strict security procedure called the 'No lone zone'. In effect, no one could go close to the weapon alone and must always be accompanied. The Americans were very strict about this and insisted on a yellow line painted on the concrete around the bomb bay and crew entrance area of each aircraft. They even had armed guards who would cock their guns if you crossed the line alone. There was a regular training programme for the loading teams who were required to be certified by the Americans before being able to load a live weapon. There were exams to be taken and snap checks of our ability to complete a load safely in a set time. All of this was called TD21 (Training Directive 21) the approved training standard required to load the 2100lb Thermo-Nuclear weapons that we were handling.

Once I had been trained up and certified I was in the thick of it. When the siren sounded, which it did quite regularly, we all dashed off to the 14 Sqdn Armament section to await instructions. As the aircraft were towed out onto the flight line and made ready, we would start our loading procedure, all closely watched by the American guards. The task entailed jacking the aircraft main wheels up off the ground and locking the jacks to prevent them sinking down. The 2100lb bomb was then released from American custody and wheeled under the bomb bay where we would hoist it up and latch it to the bomb beam in the bomb bay. A variety of checks were completed and on command, we all left the bomb bay at the same time to preserve the no lone zone. Then it was back to the crew room for a cup of tea and a break, or sometimes detailed to start on the next aircraft. If there was a break in operations while the aircraft flew, we often got away for a meal before returning ready for the next loading to take place. At 'End Ex' it was usually back to bed if the alert had been at night or back to our normal jobs if it were during the day.

After a few months I was promoted to sergeant, an event that allowed me to use the Sergeants' Mess and I was introduced there by Bob Ashley along with Roy Ridell another corporal who had been promoted from the ejection seat bay. The other benefit of being a Senior NCO (SNCO) was that it increased my total of married quarters qualifying points and I was soon allocated a house in the married quarters of RAF Wildenrath. Once we had moved into No.74 Airmen's Married Quarters (AMQ), life changed quite considerably. We were now able to accommodate guests and in July 1966 Pauline's sister Barbara and her family came to stay for a holiday. We were also so much closer to the station facilities such as the NAAFI, Astra Cinema and all the clubs and social facilities that were available. Whilst still a corporal I had been selected for the station swimming team for an event at RAF Gutesloh. This was a chance to have a look at another aspect of the RAF in Germany and to gain a few more swimming trophies.

The promotion also meant a new duty as Orderly Sergeant (OS) that came around once in while. This entailed accompanying the Orderly Officer around the Airmen's Mess to check for any complaints, taking the defaulters parade at the Guardroom, raising and lowering the RAF Ensign at the appointed hour and locking up the Sergeants' Mess at night etc. This last task caused me a problem one morning. There was a late night 'do' on at the Sergeants' Mess and it was in the early hours of the morning before I got the mess locked and to bed in the OS bunk. Unfortunately, I failed to hear my alarm clock in the morning and arrived ten minutes late at the flagpole to put up the RAF ensign. Worse still the Station Warrant Officer had noticed and called me in afterwards for a right roasting. But nothing came of it because he had been at the Mess 'do' and was probably one of the last to leave anyway.

Wildenrath swimming team 1966 - Author front row 1st from left

There were also other duties to do such as Duty Armourer (DA) that entailed being the duty person for 24 hours. In particular this involved taking charge of all the arms in the small arms store, a task that meant counting every one before taking over. Occasionally, we would be required to do two weeks on QRA duty to supplement the manpower of the 14 Sqdn plumbers. This was a boring time, although we were allowed out of the compound once a day. There was nothing much to do all day, except the routine of the daily aircraft inspection. That of course was unless an emergency was declared when it was all hands to the pumps. The aircrew lived in their flying clothing and raced out to their aircraft while the ground crews got the gates open and the aircraft ready to start engines and taxi. Luckily, while I was in the compound we only had the odd practice to deal with.

British Forces in Germany (BFG) had the benefit of very cheap petrol in the form of coupons that could be cashed in at BP garages. I joined the Motor Club, a useful facility that had a workshop where members could work on their cars in the warmth of a large garage. In order to get extra petrol coupons I bought an old Fiat 600 car that needed quite a lot of work to make it roadworthy. To have a car registered for BFG number plates and cheap petrol it had to be tested by the station MT section. This was quite a rigorous test and particularly the brake test that required all four wheels to lock when the brakes were applied. One of the dodges to pass this was to pump the tyres up to a very high pressure; my Fiat easily passed that test. Much of the floor had rusted away and I was able to repair this by riveting in a shelf from a steel locker, and one night whilst on DA duty I used the clean conditions of the Bomb Carrier bay to paint the whole car cream. A couple of years later I saw this car parked at RAF Coltishall, someone had continued with my work and even managed to register it in the UK.

There was also a Motor Club clubhouse with a lounge bar and this became a place that we often visited and made new friends. It was here that I became involved in rallying, a very popular activity with BFG personnel, and I acted as a navigator for a chap with a rear engine Renault 1100. The only problem was that these cars are very light at the front end and we had to overcome this by loading several filled sandbags into the boot at the front. Before we learnt this trick we often had near misses with the ditches on the corners. However, I found that navigating made me carsick in spite of taking medication and I decided to try my hand at driving. When I had found a spare navigator we teamed up and I took my Viva on the various events. I soon learnt all the notation required for navigation notes, tulip symbols, herringbone routes and spot references etc. well enough in fact to plan and organise a successful rally myself.

The Motor Club decided that a club shop would be a useful asset and I volunteered to get one organised. A room in the club's garage was set aside and I went about getting stocked up. From a firm in the UK I was able to send for parcels of items such as sparking plugs, seat belts and a wide variety of accessories at a very good discount and postage paid. I arranged to buy Goodyear tyres at a good discount from a dealer in Holland just across the nearby border and two of the members set up as tyre fitters (for a small fee). From a local garage trade supplier, I was able to buy spare parts to order for a wide range of cars, all at a good discount price. The local Duckhams agent let me buy 45-gallon drums of oil that I sold by the litre at a price cheaper than was available in the NAAFI. One of the main benefits I arranged was to be able to purchase goods

VAT free, thus making our spares cheaper than they could be bought locally. Although I didn't learn to speak fluent German, I soon learnt a lot of the names of car parts, such as kupplung (clutch), bremse (brakes) and auspuff (exhaust) etc. I opened the shop two or three times a week and members would come in to purchase items or place orders that I would put on my purchasing list. The shop expanded for the rest of my time at Wildenrath and I handed it over as a good non-profit-making facility when I left.

After about a year I was moved to the Bomb Dump, run by Ch/Tech John Andrews. Every morning we assembled at the Armament Sqn HQ and were transported to the other side of the airfield in a Magirus Deutz truck. This was quite familiar work to me, although the stores we maintained were a little different. The Canberra's engines are started with a large cartridge and with two squadrons flying every day there was a constant stream of starter cartridges to be delivered. Then there was a special practice bomb for the LABS bombing training, these were sheet metal steel cylinders with fins, a flat nose and a flash cartridge inside that we fitted before issue. No.14 Sqn used 20 mm ammunition in their gunpacks that were fitted whenever they undertook air firing practice. No.17 Sqn did a lot of night photography and needed boxes of illuminating flares to be delivered.

Every once in awhile a Weapons Meet would take place. This was a competition between 2 ATAF squadrons in gunnery and bombing contests for accuracy. It was Wildenrath's turn to stage the event and we in the Bomb Dump provided storage space for all the strange armaments of the foreign visitors. It was quite hard work supplying everyone with their needs but one Air Force in particular made quite an impact. Whereas most countries provided their squadrons with modern ammunition and practice bombs that went bang or flash on the target, the Belgians arrived with a truckload of their stores. We asked them what type of facility was required and they said none and proceeded to unload the truck just outside the bomb dump gate. First they threw off all the bombs. They looked just like 5-gallon oil drums with fins attached, then they tipped off a pile of sand and poured it into the bombs. It seems that when these practice bombs were dropped they burst open on impact and the sand marked the spot to be recorded for the accuracy checks. Needless to say, they didn't get a very high score, most of the bomb fins had been bent in transit. But it was quite a talking point at the all nations party we had in the Sergeants' Mess at the end of the meet.

Badge of the 6th Allied Forces Weapons Meet

Pauline was due to have our first child in April 1967 and my mother had come out on holiday to be there for the event. We went out most days to show her a little of the German countryside and culture and decided to go to see the tulips at Keukenhof in Holland. Pauline decided not to come so I took my mother there for the day, leaving Pauline in the hands of our neighbours and friends

Sgt Fred Knox and his wife Joan. On our return Pauline said she had had a few pangs and in the evening I took her to the RAF Hospital at Wegberg and left her there for the night. She had Susan at 0800 hours the next day. I knew that she'd had the baby because I woke up at precisely that time with a pain in my ankle!

Pauline and I had previously bought some camping equipment in order to tour around Europe while we were at Wildenrath. Quite modest really, a small bivouac two-man tent, lilos, sleeping bags, gas stove and that sort of thing. Once Susan was on the scene we decide to continue the camping outings and took her with us in a carrycot to a wide variety of places and countries. We got quite good at feeding and nappy changing at the side of the road and usually took the opportunity to brew up whenever we were making a bottle up for her. Generally we would go on leave in the UK to visit the family during the winter months and spent the summer touring the countries of Europe. In the three years we were at Wildenrath we visited 13 different countries, generally camping on the excellent sites that were available everywhere.

Rough and ready camping in Germany

The following year I moved to another job, this time to run the TD21 training programme. By now the American weapon that was being used had been changed to a 1650lb version, but the procedures were practically the same. There were two of us running the programme, Sgt John Richie and myself. He being the senior sergeant was nominally in charge and undertook most of the training, whereas I assisted and looked after all the sets of loading equipment that were stored on individual hand trolleys in the 14 Sqdn hanger. I undertook routine maintenance of the various items such as jacks, clamps, hand tools and work schedules etc., keeping them in top readiness for when the siren sounded. Between us we trained and tested each of the loading teams, arranging for a non-flying aircraft to be available whenever required and liaising with the American evaluation personnel. Although we each had our own loading teams, as soon as an alert or exercise was finished we could not finish as it was up to us to get the loading kits sorted out and in a fully serviceable state for the next time the siren went. Sometimes this would be only an hour or so after the previous 'Endex' had been announced, meaning we would have to work right through until the job was completed.

Showing Susan a Canberra B(I)8

In my last year in Germany I ordered a brand new tax-free right-hand drive Ford Cortina estate car through a garage in Holland for £666. Just before delivery was due I drove the Viva to the UK and met the Motor Club shop suppliers that I had been dealing with in London. They had kindly arranged for me to go to a second-hand car dealer who would buy the car from me for cash, although I do not remember how much I got for it. But the deal was done and I went back to Dover on the train. Down at the ferry terminal I walked up and down the line of cars looking for a lift and saw a BFG car with a lone friendly looking chap driving. He agreed to give me lift back to Wildenrath although he was a pilot from RAF Bruggen nearby. I had the cash in my pocket and at the time there was a £25 restriction on currency exports. Luckily I got through OK with no questions asked. Back at Wildenrath I had a buyer for the Fiat, so on the appointed day, the new owner took Pauline, Susan and I to the garage in Holland. The new car was just what we needed as an expanding family, but the real bonus was that after ordering the car the £ had been devalued quite considerably. When I came to pay the balance of the price agreed, the price of the car had also gone down quite considerably and I was left with more cash than I had calculated.

As the end of this very interesting tour approached we applied for a posting to East Anglia and were pleased to get RAF Coltishall in Norfolk. But first we had the business of preparing our married quarter for what is known as march out. This is the formal hand over when everything is inspected, the inventory checked and any damages noted. The inspection is a very strict affair and everywhere is expected to be spotless on the day. Whereas in previous years we had travelled home for Christmas, in 1968 we were in the process of cleaning our married quarter and packing up our things. We spent a quiet Christmas Day at Wildenrath and went to our very good friends Fred and Joan Knox for tea and a bit of a celebration.

I had booked a few days in the Family Transit accommodation and on the morning of the march out, Pauline and I went around to ensure everything was spick and span. Although it was winter we had let the central heating coke boiler out during the night so that in the morning we could empty the ashes and wash it out for good measure. We had spent many hours cleaning the cooker, oven and the pots and pans, vacuuming the bases of the three piece suite and, at the appointed hour, we were complimented on having a very clean house.

As part of our camping equipment I'd had a special long roof rack made for the Cortina consisting of two racks welded together end to end. So in early January 1969 we loaded everything aboard and set off back to the UK and our next posting. It was a particularly rough crossing that day, the first time we had ever felt sea sick on the ferry. But we got to Dover OK and travelled up to my mother's house at Bentley in Suffolk for our first stop.

9. Coltishall

We stayed at my mother's house for a few days before travelling up to Staffordshire. It was the middle of January, snow was forecast and we set off as soon as we could. On the way the snow started to fall very heavily and the roads started to get rather slippery. I drove steadily on and at one point some fool came speeding past as if there was no problem. But just a few miles up the road we came across him in the falling snow in the middle of the road frantically waving his arms for us to slow down. He had come to a halt on a hill with no traction and couldn't continue. As for us, with the big roof rack fully loaded we had plenty of weight to give us grip and we sailed past him with no problem, never to be seen again.

We spent our 60-day's leave visiting friends and relations and introducing Susan to the family, spending most of our time in Suffolk or in Staffordshire with Pauline's family. At the end of January 1969 I set out from Staffordshire to my new job at RAF Coltishall about eight miles north of Norwich, settling into the Sergeants' Mess for a few weeks unaccompanied, while I awaited a married quarter. Every weekend I travelled back to Staffordshire after work on Friday and returned on Sunday evening getting to know the road very well.

RAF Coltishall was home to No 226 Operational Conversion Unit (OCU) flying a variety of English Electric Lightning types, The Battle of Britain Memorial Flight and an Air Sea Rescue Flight. I was employed in the Ejection Seat Bay based in the Armament HQ building under Ch/Tech Alan Windebank. From my previous postings I was quite familiar with this type of work and soon learnt the various seat marks that were fitted to the Lightning. Although our workspace was quite cramped, we had a separate storage area for the seats as they passed in and out of the bay. We also had a lecture room where we had a training ejection seat and gave lectures and demonstrations to visitors and those who needed to know as part of their work. I particularly enjoyed this part of the work, meeting a wide variety of people and gaining more and more knowledge about ejection seats and their workings.

As usual there were other duties to perform when the siren sounded and at Coltishall this meant arming the aircraft with missiles. Although this was a training unit, it was also part of the front line defence of the UK and all the aircraft could be used for missile deployment. This was my first encounter with Air to Air Guided Weapons (AAGW) and was a whole new part of being a plumber. As usual we were formed into teams to load the Redtop or Firestreak missiles that were supplied by the personnel of the Missile Servicing Flight (MSF).

Lightning Flight Line RAF Coltishall

These are heat seeking weapons that once fired from the aircraft track the heat of the target before detonating a war head encased in steel, producing shrapnel that can rip an aircraft to shreds. Firestreak uses ammonia as the coolant for the heat seeking guidance head, had a range of four miles and could only be used for rear attacks. It was powered by a cordite motor and had infra red proximity fuse windows around the body. Red Top was a much improved version of the Firestreak using pure air to cool the guidance head, was much more sensitive, had a range of nearly seven miles and could be fired on a collision course attack.

It was the usual thing when everything had been loaded, it was time for a quick cup of tea etc. before the next wave of loading commenced. When Endex was announced we all stood down and either went to bed or back to our normal work depending on the time of day.

After two months I was allocated a married quarter and we moved into No. 66 Cromes Crescent, one of the old terrace type houses that was still decorated with camouflage paint from WWII. Next door lived Alan and Marlene Windebank, and two doors down was Sgt Mick Wright and his family, another one of the ejection seat bay personnel. Our friends Bill and Pat Paice, with whom we had travelled home from Malta, were also resident in the Coltishall married quarters, but within a few days of us moving in, they were posted off to Germany and we never saw them again. But we settled down in our new home making new friends and starting new interests to occupy our time.

There was a very good nursery school on the station and Pauline soon got Susan enrolled. The building was quite close to the Armament HQ building and this was quite useful, because at lunchtimes I was able to pick her up on my bicycle on the way home. We also used the swimming pool quite extensively and, after passing a life saving test (I was already at Bronze Medallion level anyway), was able to sign the key out any time I wished. We were able to have the pool practically to ourselves at times and by the time Susan was 4 years old I had taught her to swim. In the evenings many of the wives worked in the local baked bean canning factory at North Walsham for a bit of extra money and as a social occasion. Pauline joined them on a regular basis and got to know many more friends at the same time.

In 1953 I had signed on for 12 years service from my 18th birthday and in 1966 when this was completed I re-engaged for a further 10 years to put me into line for a pension. It was now 1969 and I realised that I may soon be coming to the end of my service with no formal qualifications. I had left school before taking any examinations and the only qualification I had was the certificate awarded to me on completion of my armament engineering apprenticeship at RAF Halton. There was a very good education section at RAF Coltishall and I decided to sign up for some evening classes and take a few GCE O level exams. First I had a go at English Language and passed the exam in November 1969. This seemed to be quite easy and next I had a go at Mathematics and Geometrical and Mechanical Drawing, passing the exams in June 1970. Next I thought I would have a go at the General Paper, an examination requiring two essays from a choice of subjects. When I opened my question paper there were several choices and I picked 'Describe the workings of an Internal Combustion Engine' a task I found very easy. The other choice I picked was 'The future role of the RAF'. This took a bit of thinking about but I wrote of the reduced use of pilots for combat and the increasing use of guided missiles and unmanned aircraft. This produced another pass in November 1970. Finally I went for Geography and Physics gaining passes in June 1971.

Lightning landing at RAF Coltishall

In September 1970 RAF Coltishall staged a Battle of Britain Open Day, an event that we all took part in, preparing displays and manning the various stands and exhibits. The Armament HQ was thrown open to the public to view the various pieces of equipment we had on show and we gave demonstrations of our work and lectures to all those who turned up. One of the big events of the day was a diamond 16 fly-past consisting of Lightning aircraft in a diamond formation. A great deal of time and effort was put into preparing the 16 aircraft plus a few spares for the day and the spectacular fly past took place as scheduled. The participants then started to come in to land in front of the crowd but unfortunately one of them suffered brake problems, burst a tyre and blocked the runway. The remaining aircraft were then diverted to RAF Wattisham for the time being. Once the runway was cleared after a couple of hours the aircraft returned but just before landing, T4 Lightning XM 990 developed problems and crashed just off the A1140 Norwich to South Walsham road very close to the village of Little Plumstead. Luckily, the two pilots ejected safely with minor injuries and were picked up by the Air Sea Rescue helicopter. After a few days they both came in to the seat bay to thank us for our work and handed over the traditional crate of beer. Later we each received a letter of thanks from the Engineering Squadron Commander, a document I still have and prize today.

Living in the heart of Broadland was ideal and provided plenty of opportunity for us to become tourists when off duty and make the most of the countryside. My mother only lived an hour's drive away and we visited her regularly at weekends or she came to stay with us when there were events on such as open days. Pauline's family was also able to come and stay with us for holidays and we took them for trips on the Broads or to Cromer and the coast. Wroxham was just down the road and I often drove there to visit the bank in the village. Our weekly shop was a trip into Norwich, a place that we got to know and love and still enjoy visiting. One of the plumbers I worked with lived in Norwich and his wife worked at the Startrite shoe factory. This was a very useful connection as we were able to buy plenty of good quality shoes for Susan at very cheap staff discount prices.

Meanwhile back in the seat bay, Alan Windebank had completed his service in the RAF and left, Mick Wright had been posted and I was left in charge. We had been pressing for a larger area in which to work. The workshop bay was very cramped and we felt like sardines every time we had to move seats around. The seat storage area was in one of the three large bays of the building and in order to keep dust off the serviced seat structures, I had manufactured a number of fitted polythene covers. This was taken a step further by the powers-that-be and they asked if we would like the ends of the large bay to be filled in with partition walls. From this I was able to assist with a design project for a completely new ejection seat servicing bay that would be reasonably dust free and with plenty of space. Once the walls had been completed and the whole thing decorated we moved in and set up shop in much better conditions. Unfortunately, it was deemed that servicing the 'instruments' as they were known had to be undertaken in another room that was even more dust free, but we were allocated a space close to the end of our new bay. The 'instruments' were the parts of the ejection seat that contained timers, barometric devices and other clockwork trains such as the drogue gun and barometric release unit. These all had to be stripped, oiled, reassembled and timed or tested before being refitted to the seat structure.

Once again Pauline and I decided to go for another overseas posting and this time I applied for Gibraltar, Cyprus or Hong Kong. The beauty of the RAF in those days was that there were still plenty of overseas bases still open where families and children could also be accommodated. When the posting came through we were very pleased to find that we had got Cyprus and would be travelling in August 1971. It was now time to set about preparing for the move.

The first item was the Cortina Estate car that we needed to sell before leaving for Cyprus. I had modified it a little and added a few extras that would not have helped in the sale or increased the value. I had fitted it with a set of wide wheels and tyres and managed to find someone at Coltishall with a Cortina that wanted them. So for the agreed price we swapped our wheels and tyres over. I had also modified the front grill with two spot lamps inserted alongside the headlamps and black matt paint over the chrome. To sort this out I got hold of a second-hand grill from a scrap dealer and sold off the spot lamps and the long roof rack separately. With that completed I advertised the car in the local press and was able to get my asking price.

It was now time to get the married quarter prepared for hand over and we went through the usual routine to get it spick and span for march out. Without a car it was not a problem living on camp with all the facilities, but we did want to visit our families before we left and the only alternative was the train. We travelled to Staffordshire by the cross-country route from Norwich changing at Ely, Peterborough, Nuneaton and Stafford to reach Stone. After a weekend there saying farewell to everyone we travelled back by the same route, using a taxi for the last leg from Norwich station. We also took a ride on the train to Ipswich to visit my mother, but that was a little more straight forward and we were able to catch a bus to Bentley and back to Ipswich to catch the return train to Norwich.

On 10 August 1971, the morning of the march out, we were up very early putting the finishing touches to our packing and cleaning. At the appointed hour Pauline and Susan were allowed to sit in the front room of our married quarter while the march out inspection and inventory check took place. The inspecting officer complimented Pauline and, after signing a few forms, it was all over and we boarded the transport with our luggage for our journey to Norwich Station. The train ride took us via London to RAF Brize Norton in Oxfordshire, the RAF's equivalent of an airport, for our evening flight to Cyprus.

10. Akrotiri

At Brize Norton we entered the Air Terminal building and checked in just like at a civilian airport, all very efficient and modern. We weren't due to fly out until quite late that evening so settled down for a meal and a few hours waiting. Later that night at about 2300 hours we were called to board our aircraft, a Britannia turbo prop known as the whispering giant. The flight to Cyprus was quite uneventful, and much more comfortable than the old Hastings I had travelled on in the past. We landed at RAF Akrotiri at about 0700 hours on 11 August 1971 and as we came down the steps onto the Tarmac the heat hit us. Even at that time of the day, August in Cyprus is extremely hot if you have just arrived from the UK.

We were met at the air terminal by Ch/T Wally Wooldridge our appointed plumber minder who took us to the Astir Hotel in Limassol. We were given a pack of information and a family room to relax in for the rest of the day. The room was extremely hot as we tried to sleep, even though it was supposedly air-conditioned. We even tried opening the windows for some cool air, but of course this made it worse and the hotel staff laughed at us. The next morning we were taken on a tour of private properties that were available for rent in Limassol in order that we could select somewhere to live. We opted for a nice little bungalow in Spiro Stathopoulou Street, signed the necessary agreement paperwork and paid a deposit during the afternoon. Our taxi driver then took us back to the hotel where we picked up our luggage before being dropped off at our new home.

It was now evening and while Pauline unpacked and cleaned where necessary, I went into Limassol to buy some groceries and bits and pieces that we needed. I noted as carefully as I could where our house was situated but on the way back I got lost and couldn't find my way home. I wandered up and down, asked a few people if they knew where Spiro Stathapolou Street was, but to no avail. In the end I resorted to taking a taxi, the driver seeming to know where I wanted to go, but even he couldn't find the place. But he asked various people that he seemed to know until in the end we came across a policeman who gave him directions. He eventually dropped me off at my new home, rather later than I had anticipated and to Pauline's relief because I had been away so long.

The next day we decided to buy a car and I went along to a nearby dealer that had been recommended in the RAF welcoming pack. The little Renault 4 seemed to be a very popular car on the island and I picked out a nice little white one that was only one year old and in good order. I was able to transfer the insurance cover I'd had for the Cortina through the local General Accident office the same day and drove the car home. The Renault 4 was known as a 'Bondu Basher' by the island's service personnel and it certainly lived up to this name. During our three years in Cyprus we loaded it up with roof rack, pram and beach equipment and went to all the outlying points of the island including the rough tracks that served as roads in many parts. Because it was a small four-door estate car it was very versatile, with the dash mounted gear lever, bench front seat and fold down rear seat, it really was a family holdall.

After my two days of settling in time and a weekend, I reported for duty at RAF Akrotiri. Once I had completed my arrival procedure I was given a job in the Bomb Dump with Wally Wooldridge in charge; this was another familiar role and I was soon actively involved. Akrotiri was home to Vulcan bombers, supersonic Lightnings, Hercules transports, and Whirlwind SAR helicopters. Passing through were all the transport aircraft such as VC10s, Britannias and a wide range of other visitors. It was also the temporary base for a variety of visiting squadrons on Armament Practice Camp (APC) taking advantage of the good weather. We handled a very wide variety of armament stores to supply all these aircraft and I was soon getting acclimatised in the heat.

Several of us who had been on the BD course and were qualified were formed into a team to deal with a variety of tasks associated with that type of work. By now the name Bomb Disposal had been changed and it was now called Explosives Ordnance Disposal (EOD) and becoming more and more important on RAF stations.

All the time-expired and unserviceable stores were regularly taken out to sea and dumped using an Army landing craft, but first they had to be prepared. To ensure that the various items would sink and be attacked by the seawater we laboriously emptied the boxes and containers and made holes in appropriate places before repacking them. We occasionally went out on to the Larnaca bombing range to dispose of various stores that had failed to explode or to repair the targets once the aircraft had finished their bombing or gunnery sorties. If it was a good day we would take a 1000lb bomb out for a demolition exercise, an opportunity to try out our low order detonation skills. This operation cracks open the bomb case with explosive, but not enough to explode the whole thing and needing good judgement to determine how much explosive to use.

We often got called out to flares and other items washed up on the long coastline around Akrotiri, usually these were expended and rarely a threat.

Preparing a 1000lb bomb for test demolition on the Larnaca Range

~ RAF Plumber ~

After about two months I was moved to the Armament Squadron's Ground Equipment Servicing Section as NCO i/c and inventory holder. I was to be promoted to Ch/T and take over from Ch/T Derek Howarth, who was at the end of his tour and due to return to the UK. There was a workforce of a sergeant and two SAC armourers, a corporal and a J/T ground equipment fitters, and two civilian labourers. The section serviced the wide variety of armament handling equipment held on the station and any other similar work that was allocated. This included, Red Top and Firestreak missile cradles and transporters, Standard Airfield Bomb Transporters (SABTs), Type F Bomb Trolleys, Alvis bomb loading trolleys for the Canberras, Vulcan bomb loading kits consisting of power packs and jacks, Type R loaders and a range of hoists and static ground equipment. As NCO i/c I took over the huge inventory and was the 'proud owner' of all this equipment, two canvas hangers, a large quantity of steel tubing for targets and a multitude of tools and workshop equipment.

Once my promotion came through it put me up to the top of the married quarters list and I was allocated a 'hiring' at No.3 Aristoteli Valouriti Street in north eastern Limassol. A 'hiring' is a civilian flat or house rented from the owner by the RAF, the service occupant paying normal married quarter charges to the RAF. Our new home was a very spacious two-bedroom bungalow with a garage, garden and front balcony. On the roof was a solar powered water heater and in the garden a swing. The house was so big that the furniture we were allocated did not fill the place so we hired some extra pieces from a local dealer on a monthly rental basis. Susan started going to the local British Forces Primary School in Limassol and I bought myself a Yamaha 75 motor bike to get back and forth to work, thus enabling Pauline to get around and to and from Akrotiri when she wanted. In our spare time we set about visiting every point of the island that we could get to in our Bondu Basher, a period that would luckily take us to places that later would have been out of the question. We went right up the Pan Handle, the long Peninsula to the north east, visited all the Roman antiquity sites, up to St. Helarion castle, Troodos Mountains when the snow was on the ground and anywhere that was of interest.

No.3 Aristoteli Valouriti Street, Limassol

In December 1971 I was given the opportunity to do a detachment in the Persian Gulf, the only time I was able to leave the island in three years. I was to go to RAF Masirah to do a survey on some ground equipment there. A flight in a C130 Hercules and an entry visa were arranged and I climbed aboard with my kit. On board were a Mobile Air Movements (MAMs) team with some empty horse transportation crates and a pongo Corporal of Horse. Although it is impossible to talk while airborne because of the noise of the engines, I managed to find out that they were going to transport some race horses for a local Sheikh. The pongo was aboard with a humane killer, just in case the horses tried to bolt while airborne. I had come prepared with a set of ear defenders as I had been warned of the noise. But the MAMs team really had it organised, as soon as we had taken off they unrolled their sleeping bags, donned their ear defenders and settled down in the quietest part of the fuselage, up on the tail ramp. At Masirah I spent a few days surveying SABTs and a Vulcan bomb loading power pack, kept there for operational emergencies. In the evenings I chatted to the station's permanent staff in the NAAFI and drinking Tiger Beer, a nice reminder of Singapore. I was able to get out to a local village where I bought two Maria Theresa Thalers that I took home for souvenirs. My trip back was a lot more comfortably; I travelled in an empty Queen's Flight Mk 1 Andover. It had transported the then Prime Minister Edward Heath to somewhere in the world and had landed at Masirah to refuel on its return. I sat in the PMs seat for the whole trip, drank coffee from china cups and ate biscuits from a china plate, all decorated with the RAF crest. The best in-flight catering I have ever had.

Life was really great now, we were on a holiday island with loads of facilities and a nice big house to live in. My mother came out on holiday in April 1972, and as we picked her up from Nicosia airport, I started feeling rather rough. After a few days I was diagnosed with mumps, one of the most painful and uncomfortable experiences I have ever had. But I got over it in time to take my mother back to the airport for her flight home. When I eventually reported back to work, I was able to cancel the leave I'd had while I'd been ill. Pauline had been able to show mother around while I had been in bed and it didn't spoil her holiday too much.

I had heard all about the Water Ski Club at Akrotiri from my friends at work and in early 1972 we decided to join. The Western Cyprus Services Water Ski Club (WCSWSC) was situated on the Limassol Bay side of the Akrotiri Peninsula next to the sailing club. Once I had joined we spent most of our spare time there and I would meet Pauline and Susan there after work to enjoy the cooler evenings and the water sport. There was a small NAAFI canteen plus all the usual paraphernalia of a jetty, ski boats, skiing equipment, slalom course, ski jump and swimming raft just off-shore. It didn't take me long to learn to ski, first on two skis and later on one ski. Then I learnt to drive the ski boats and took turns towing the members and visitors on whatever trip they fancied. Next I got myself checked out as an instructor, teaching new skiers wet drill (basic instruction) and then taking them out on the water behind a boat. Eventually, I became a committee member and volunteered as Beach Member, a post responsible for all the beach facilities, the jetty, raft, buildings and the car park.

This was really heaven and apart from work, a permanent holiday during the summer months. Pauline was able to sit on the club patio in the shade socialising with all the other members and having a go at snorkelling in the clear water when she wanted to cool down. Susan made many new friends with the other children and spent most of the time out on the raft learning to dive and swim expertly. She was so enthusiastic about swimming that we enrolled her with the Tadpoles, the Akrotiri swimming club for youngsters. She soon passed all her distance badges and before she was 7-years old was awarded her one mile certificate and badge.

But I still had to go to work, we worked out in the open most of the time and soon got used to the hot sun every day. We had a steady input of servicing work all the time, but it was not boring, as we were out and about with the tractor, towing equipment around the station much of the time. One day I was in the workshop office updating records when there was a crash and a scream outside. I rushed out to find out what was going on only to find Ted Angus our J/T ground equipment fitter lying on the floor with blood pouring from a gash in his forehead. It seems he had hit his thumb with a hammer and the pain had made him pass out. When he came round two of us loaded him into the section minibus and rushed him up to the Station Sick Quarters (SSQ). By now he had revived somewhat and as we led him in, a nurse looked at the blood pouring down his face and asked what the problem was. Of course his answer was that he had hit his thumb with a hammer, causing everyone to burst out laughing, including Ted who could now see the funny side of it.

But the old secondary duties were always calling us to do other things. The main bomb load of the Vulcans was 21x1000lb bombs loaded on three seven-store bomb carriers. It could also carry a 950lb Thermo Nuclear device and I was drafted in to one of the loading teams. With the aid of a hydraulic power pack the bomb load is hoisted up into the bomb bay using two hydraulic jacks that extend to the roof of the bomb bay. I was given the power pack operators post, working a lever either side controlling each jack and it was up to me to raise or lower the load on instruction from the team leader. Of course we regularly had to practice this and it gave us an interesting break from normal work and a close up view of a Vulcan.

Vulcan at IWM Duxford

At the end of October 1972 I was allocated a married quarter on Akrotiri and we moved up into No.17 Albion Street, a nice comfortable semi-detached two-bedroom house with a garden and a small balcony. And of course we were much closer to all the base facilities that previously we had to travel to and, as many of our friends were already in married quarters, this provided quite a social ring of plumbers wives and families. During the winter of 1972/73 there was much work to do down at the ski club and, although skiing had finished for the season, many of our friends were committee members. We spent quite a lot of time there servicing boats, repairing equipment, improving the facilities and generally getting ready for the following season.

Skiing started again in April and Pauline was due to have our second child at Akrotiri hospital in early May. She was due to go into hospital on the first Sunday in May at 1100 hours and as usual we all went down to the ski club at 0700 hours to catch the calm water. But this time not only did we take all our picnic gear for the day but also all the things she would need in hospital. At the appointed hour we headed off to the hospital, leaving Susan behind with friends at the ski club. Once Pauline was installed in a hospital bed I said goodbye and headed off back to the ski club for the rest of the day skiing. The next day, Monday 7th May, I had arranged to visit Pauline late in the afternoon and as I walked in the nurse pointed me towards my new daughter Katie. Pauline had only just given birth and I was there practically within a few minutes. Back at work there was much congratulating, joking about baby plumbers, new ski club members and presents from our friends. One of the lads, Sgt Jim Jarvie even made a miniature baby size water ski that we still have on display in our lounge today.

Pauline and Susan at Troodos

My mother had remarried in August 1973 and a few months after Katie arrived she came out to stay with us on honeymoon with my new stepfather, Wilf Read. I hired the station recreational VW minibus for two weeks and after collecting them from Nicosia airport, we spent a wonderful time touring all over the island with Katie in a carrycot on the back seat. They also spent a lot of time at the ski club and along Limassol sea front, thoroughly enjoying being taken around the sights and acquiring a taste for the very popular Panteleimon wine.

Our old friends Ch/T Fred Knox, his wife Joan and family had arrived on the island while we were still living in Limassol and we became very close. He was given the task of setting up an EOD section, to deal with all the EOD incidents and to manage the EOD kit. His team was a permanent SAC plumber and us EOD qualified plumbers who acted in a part time role when we were needed. Those of us who lived on the base were roped in for duty EOD NCO to deal with any of the out-of-hours incidents that might occur. This led to a number of interesting tasks for me, particularly at the air terminal.

Author examining demolition crater and shrapnel, Larnaca Range

My first incident occurred one evening when I was called out to what was reported to be a bomb at the air terminal. When I got there the RAF police advised me that there was a bomb in the cistern of the gent's toilet. I thought it a rather odd place to put a bomb and gingerly lifted the lid off the high level cistern. Unfortunately, I could not see in because of the low ceiling and decided to gently feel around inside. What I felt were rounds of 20 mm ammunition and managed to fish out three live rounds and get the toilet working again. Someone on APC had decided to take a souvenir home but had had second thoughts before boarding the aircraft and the possibility of being searched. The next incident was again at the air terminal, a bomb in a travel bag had been reported. When I got there the bag had been placed out on a lawn and it was up to me to deal with it. At that time we had very little equipment to deal with Improvised Explosive Devices (IEDs) and I had to do what ever I could. The lawn was in an enclosed area and I instructed the Snowdrops to keep everyone clear while I investigated. The zip was partly open and I could see wires inside and could hear the sound of ticking. The only suitable kit I had with me was the old EOD favourite, fishing line and a hook. I attached the hook to the zip, stood behind a building and pulled. Just at that moment some innocent airman came swanning round the corner having somehow got past the police cordon. But all was well, the ticking turned out to be an alarm clock and the wires a set of Christmas tree lights. Someone was probably on his or her way back to the UK minus his bag and not knowing what problems he had left behind.

We held the ski club annual championships on August Bank Holiday Monday every year and the big prize was always to become Overall Champion. Points for individual tricks, slalom and jump events were totted up to calculate the overall total and points had to be gained in each discipline. I was not so good at jumping but could just about manage to get over the jump without falling over to record a minimum distance. I was quite good at Slalom and could compete with the best but it was the tricks event that I concentrated on. I would get towed out into the bay and practice without my rivals seeing what I could do and at the championships I got the Overall Champion second place, much to the disgust of the hard men who had been concentrating on the jumps. I got a very good score in the slalom, just managed to get over the jump on my final run but won the tricks event outright. Competition was always available at the club; we had a slalom ladder screwed up on the clubhouse wall with all challengers names displayed. To climb the ladder one could challenge a person above at any time to compete on the slalom and if you won you could change places. During the 1974 season all the best skiers had gone home to the

UK and I was left at the top of the ladder being challenged by all the hopefuls below.

Slalom competition winner

One afternoon the EOD crew was called to an incident at the air terminal, this time we were told there was a civilian airliner coming in with a bomb on board. The aircraft was taxied to a safe dispersal area and all the passengers were disembarked and taken away in coaches to the air terminal. We unloaded all the baggage and set it out in rows some distance from the aircraft and left it to the Snowdrops to bring the passengers back in small groups for a baggage search. We had a break at that point, but once it was completed we started to search the fuselage of the aircraft. With the help of the crew we searched every nook and cranny for a bomb but to no avail. After a safe period of several hours it was decided to call the search off and under instruction from the crew we reloaded all baggage. The passengers climbed aboard and they took off for their destination none the worse for it. We in the meantime had learnt a few new EOD procedures.

The annual ski club championships were due to take place just under three weeks after we would have left the island at the end of our three year tour. Pauline agreed that we should stay for the extra time on leave in order that I could take part as I had a very good chance of winning 'The Overall Champion' trophy. I persuaded the authorities to delay our flight home, married quarters march out, and all that sort of thing and so everything was set

We would put our new posting to RAF Wattisham on hold even though we could at last take advantage of a real home posting. We could also move into the house we were buying from my mother in a family arrangement resulting from her wedding earlier in the year. But in mid-July the Cyprus National Guard in a coup organised in Athens deposed President Makarios and things became rather uncertain.

Within a week, Turkish armed forces invaded Cyprus to protect the safety of the Turkish Cypriots. Fierce fighting took place, while Greece attempted to reinforce the Greek Cypriot forces, meeting with failure. As the fighting erupted in Limassol British Forces families were evacuated under fire to Akrotiri and we were allocated two families to live in our house. Civilian holidaymakers were also evacuated to Akrotiri and the priority was to get them away by air before any families could be repatriated. By this time I was officially on leave and male personnel were expected to sleep at their places of work. I checked in at work and was told I was not needed and to go home. With nothing to do and a house full of families (three women and seven children) I went and enrolled at the Volunteer Centre that had been set up to organise any spare manpower. I was immediately put on the night shift as a controller, taking phone calls of requests for help, despatching working parties and generally trying to solve problems through the night. The beauty of it was that I went home in the morning and was able get into my own bed that had just been vacated by Pauline. In the evening I would report in for duty and organise such things as nappies for the married quarters, freight loading teams for the constant flow of Hercules aircraft and any other task that needed manpower.

Nicosia Airport had closed after being bombed by the Turkish Air Force and it was decided that the EOD team would go and make a start of clearing the runway of unexploded bombs and any other devices that were found. We loaded up our Land Rovers and

Trailers and set out for the airport. There was a detachment of pongos still there looking after the UK's interests and we were given a Nissen hut for accommodation. The next day we started sweeping the airfield, plotting the unexploded bombs (UXBs), recording the work that was required and assessing the situation. The first task was to clear up the UXBs. The Turkish Airforce had been using 750lb bombs with delay detonators, but because they had dropped them from low level and not high level many of the bombs had skipped off the runway and exploded in the air on the bounce. We could see this from the markings on the runway, a long scraping indentation with lines scratched either side where the tail fins touched and then several yards forward the tell tale shrapnel pock marks in the tarmac.

Burnt out Cyprus Airways Trident and EOD Landrover - Nicosia 1974

We searched all the airport buildings for UXBs and IEDs and found a few souvenirs to take home. I had a large Greek flag that I found in the Nicosia Flying Club Office and from an abandoned Greek gun emplacement two 110 mm Russian shell cases. Out on the airfield we found several 750lb UXBs, most of which had spilt casings and large quantities of ammunition cases of various calibres.

We started to dig out the explosives from the split bomb cases to make them safe, but the fumes overcame us and we all got headaches. Our CO was Flight Lieutenant Ted Costick and it was decided to carry out a low order detonation on one of these in the nearby quarry. Unfortunately, a little too much plastic explosive was used and the thing went off as a high order blast sending shrapnel flying through the trees where we stood. But no one was hit and at least we had got rid of that one.

Unexploded Turkish 750lb bomb, author left

Explosive removed from unexploded bomb

Author inspecting damage from air burst bomb

At some stage Ted Costick was recalled to Akrotiri and I was left with a small party to do a bit more clearing up work before he returned. On the second day I was woken up by one of the team at 0500 hours to say that the war had started again. It was such a shock that I puffed on a cigarette that someone handed to me even though I had especially given up for my return to the UK. The Greeks had started shelling the Turks again and some of the shots were landing close by. There was nowhere to go so we just sat tight, listened to the action and waited until it stopped. I consulted with the CO of our army friends and they managed to get me a telephone line to Akrotiri who advised me to get out as soon as possible and warned me of the possible points where the Turks may have road blocks. I stuffed my Greek flag deep into my sleeping bag in case we were searched, had a quick check to see if any of the shells in the living accommodation were unexploded and live and set off as quick as we could. On the road back we kept a look out for trouble but saw nothing whilst all the time trying to raise Akrotiri on the radio that had been out of range at Nicosia. About halfway back we made contact, a pleasant relief and we were talked back in while giving reports of what we saw on the way.

And so my part in the war came to an end, much to Pauline's relief. She had no idea what I was doing or what had become of me. Once the holidaymakers had been flown back to the UK it was the turn of the evacuated families and our guests eventually left leaving us to sort out the house ready for march out. The two 110 mm shell cases I parcelled up and sent home by post, with brass umbrella stands written on the customs labels, which I later found had done the trick. But we had a few days down at the ski club before leaving, unfortunately skiing had been abandoned during the war and of course the championships cancelled much to my bitter disappointment. We all swapped stories and had a few beers, our friends' gradually being repatriated as their turn came for a flight home. And finally it was our turn and we entered the air terminal with all the ski club members wishing us goodbye. We boarded a Britannia full of Ghurkas and left the island on 31 August 1974.

11. Wattisham Lightnings

On the flight we were given a sky cot for Katie but she didn't want to sleep and spent most of the journey crawling up and down the gangway and being fussed over by the Ghurkas. We landed at Brize Norton in the late afternoon but got held up at Customs enquiring about the long canvas bag that I was carrying. I had brought my ski home with me and the Customs Officers wanted to check it in case it was a gun. But all was well and we made it through to the arrivals hall.

Before leaving Cyprus I had ordered a new Renault 6 car to be ready upon our arrival, the deposit for this being the Bondu Basher we had traded in at the Renault dealer in Cyprus. But there was no sign of our new car and I started a series of phone calls to find out what had happened. The local Renault Dealer told me they knew nothing about it and gave me the telephone number of the main offices in London. The only information I could get there was that they had the money for the deposit but no order had been placed and I should contact them two days later when something would have been sorted out. In the end we resorted to hiring a taxi for our trip up to Staffordshire, a very lucrative trip for the unsuspecting driver.

Safely home we could now get things sorted out, the shell cases had arrived and when the local press got to hear of our arrival they published an article with a picture of Katie and Susan beside them entitled 'Souvenir of Terror'. I managed to get some sense out of the Renault organisation and after a few days was advised that my new car was ready for collection from the main dealer in the middle of London. Cadging a lift from a local lorry driver friend I got to the outskirts of the city and completed the journey by underground. Driving a brand new car in the city rush hour was a bit frightening, but once I got out onto the open road away from the heavy traffic it was easy going and no damage was done.

Katie and Susan with a 'Souvenir of Terror'

In the family house deal we had bought a complete house, 'Delphis', and its contents at Bentley from my mother and it was now ready for us just to move in. I reassembled the roof rack we had brought with us from Cyprus, a job I had expected to do at Brize Norton, loaded up the car and we all set off for Suffolk on 13 September 1974. The rest of my disembarkation leave was spent settling in, sorting everything out, getting Susan registered at the local primary school and meeting our new neighbours. In the Bentley Case is Altered pub I even met people I had known from an early age and we soon became regular village people.

We were only nine miles from RAF Wattisham and I would be able to commute to work every day. On my first day there I started my arrival procedure, including a visit to the Families Office that dealt with married quarters and all that sort of thing. I enquired about a married quarter and the clerk, who happened to be an ex-RN Captain, advised me that there were no houses available that day. But I had only made the enquiry because I wanted to claim the allowance that was available to cover legal fees if you purchased your own house when no married quarters were available. When I asked him to get the Families Officer to sign the authorisation form for me, he refused saying I wasn't entitled because a married quarter would shortly be available. But I persevered and demanded to see the Families Officer who agreed with me that as there was not a quarter available that day there was no problem with signing the form. I think the ex-RN Captain thought he was still in the service and not just a clerk now.

Wattisham was home to two squadrons of Lightnings, Nos 29 and 111 Squadrons, and a SAR Flight of helicopters. I was allocated a job in the Missile Servicing Flight (MSF), the section that dealt with all the storage, servicing and delivery of Air-to-Air Guided Weapons (AAGW), based on the other side of the airfield. In the case of Lightnings, this meant Firestreak and Red Top missiles again. Whereas I had only been employed loading them to the aircraft in the past, now it was a bit more complicated. Every missile had to be regularly dismantled, inspected, guidance systems tested, reassembled and placed back in the specially heated and secure storage sheds.

The major part of MSF was situated within a secure wire compound of several acres that could only be entered via the main gate at the Police Piquet Post. The whole area was designated an Explosives Storage Area (ESA), meaning that all unauthorised battery operated equipment, such as digital watches and radios, were banned. Smoking materials were also banned, all of which had to be left at the Piquet Post on entry; even people with heart pacemakers were not allowed in unless specially authorised. Inside the compound the buildings consisted of heated storage sheds, a large concrete explosion-proof workshop, known as 'the cathedral' and an adjoining electronics workshop. There was also a plant room to supply compressed air and emergency power, a stores building and an ammonia bay, where ammonia bottles were filled for supply to the squadrons. Outside the compound was a ground equipment servicing bay and the main HQ office block, which also included a crew room and sleeping accommodation for duty personnel.

This was like belonging to a close knit community, staffed by about forty fairies, plumbers and civilians, all concentrated on the same task of missile maintenance and storage. The CO was a Flying Officer of the Electrical Engineering Branch, while the Warrant Officer (WO) was an A.Tech(W). Because of the highly technical nature of the job, there were several Ch/Ts of both the Armament and Instrument trades. The senior Armament Ch/T was known as the Site Supervisor and was responsible for the day-to-day running of the site. Most of the technical staff worked in the cathedral or electronics workshop, but working around the site was the 'Outside Gang' lead by a corporal plumber. They were unofficially called the 'Sheddies' and were responsible for all movements of missiles and equipment around the site and for making deliveries to the squadrons on the airfield. The only other work party was the ground equipment servicing team, usually one or two plumbers and two civilian labourers.

I was set to work in the cathedral, initially servicing Red Top missiles and later also Firestreaks. Every day the MSF control staff in the HQ building would detail missiles for the Sheddies to deliver to us in the cathedral for servicing. Here they would be hoisted, using pneumatic hoists, onto an assembly rig that enabled us to dismantle and examine all the parts. The front end or guidance unit went down the corridor to the electronics workshop for the Fairies to service and test, together with a few items of wiring. The explosive parts would be examined and checked, electrical detonating parts tested with a safety ohmmeter, and an examination of the cordite rocket motor undertaken. Although we were able to use explosion-proof torches, a mains powered fibre optic light was needed to examine for cracks deep inside the cordite. This was accomplished by placing the power unit of the fibre optic outside the building with a hole drilled through the concrete blast wall for the long fibre lens to be used inside.

Once everything was ready for assembly, the parts were returned and the missile was put back together ready for testing. This was probably the most dangerous part of the whole procedure. Each missile was clamped to a test stand in a small room off the main cathedral. All the necessary connections were made to the test rig and a small door in the blast wall opposite the missile's rear end opened in case the motor fired. The operator then cleared everyone to the other side of the blast wall, sounded the alarm and undertook the test procedure. Every aspect of the weapon was tested as if it were fitted to an aircraft, including target acquisition, simulated firing, and flight, but not, of course, motor firing or warhead detonation! The missile was then reloaded to its transportation cradle and pushed outside for the Sheddies to take away.

Red Top AAGW

Our house, 'Delphis' at Station Road, Bentley, was a bit small for a growing family so we decided to extend it as soon as we could. It was a semi-detached, two-up two-down house with a bathroom over a kitchen at the rear and a conservatory. It was an ex-railway house and had been built around 1874, over a 100 years ago. I contacted the local builder who had previously put the bathroom in for my mother and he put me onto a local architect who worked for the Eastern Electricity Company and did private designs in his spare time. After measuring up and producing plans for planning permission we were all set. We got permission to build a large extension lounge with a bedroom over. By reworking the narrow stairs we finished with four bedrooms, lounge, dining room and large hall, leaving the conservatory untouched.

The extension of Delphis

I got a quote from our builder and he agreed to allow me to do much of the simple work to reduce costs. Once we had the mortgage arrangements sorted out, we were away. The builder measured out the foundations and I put in several days' hard slog digging them all out to the correct depth. Once the foundations were in, the builder started work on building the walls and knocking down the sections that were not required. There wasn't much I could do at this stage except go to work every day and clear up in evenings when I came home. As usual with all builders, they kept rushing off to other jobs and there were some considerably frustrating delays that were even more worrying as often the weather was bad and the wind would be rushing through the skeleton of the house.

But we had one bedroom upstairs and one room downstairs that remained untouched and we made the most of it. As work progressed I was able to do all the interior woodwork except the windows, all the electrical wiring except in the extension, install a complete open fire central heating system, and all the decorating. Eventually it was finished and the builders left so that we could now complete the changes and finish off the final touches to our nice big family house.

Not long after arriving at Wattisham I was sent on a Red Top and Firestreak course at RAF Newton near Nottingham. This was a fascinating place with many examples of guided weapons past, experimental and present on display. The ten-day course gave me the training I needed to qualify for the QRTFX annotation to my trade achievements. When I went back to Wattisham to put all this into practice, I was primarily employed on the Red Tops but occasionally had to service Firestreaks if the regular team were on leave etc. I hated these old missiles, they were held together with hundreds of screws that had luting, a type of putty, pressed into all the cracks and joints to make them water proof; once the luting had hardened they were difficult to dismantle. Reassembly was just as bad because all the old luting had to be removed and then replaced with fresh once all the screws were back in place. On the Red Top however, all the sections (guidance, warhead, motor) were all connected with torque loaded clamping rings and seals, a much easier job.

During alerts and exercises we continued to work with the missiles, mainly moving them around receiving them back into store and rectification, whilst also defending the perimeter fence against attack. At such times we usually worked shifts of 12 hours on and 12 hours off and I was usually able to get home when off shift. At the time, Russian Bears (bomber aircraft) were continuously probing our air defences as part of the Cold War and Wattisham Lightnings often took off from the QRA sheds to intercept them. One day at the local hairdressers, Pauline told me that two Lightnings had screamed low overhead, heading out to sea. The ladies, knowing I was in the RAF, complained to her about the noise. But when she explained how the Russians were testing us, they accepted the noise and did not complain again.

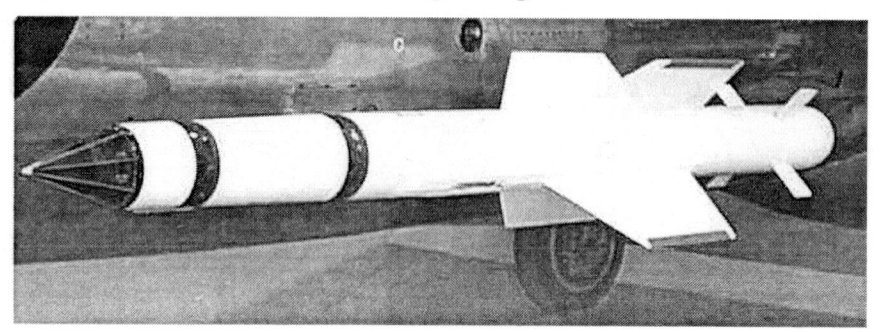

Firestreak AAGW

After extending the house, the next thing to do was the garden. My mother was an avid gardener and the flowerbeds were immaculate. But I wanted a vegetable plot and my gaze fell on a piece of the old Bentley station railway yard next door. It was actually at a lower level than our garden, down an embankment of ash. This was where the engine for the Hadleigh branch line had been kept and every day they had raked out the ashes and built up the bank. The track bed had long gone and the station was now closed, but the land was not really suitable for a garden. However, I contacted British Rail to enquire if I could rent a section, and for a few pounds a year we had a garden plot and somewhere to park our car.

But much work was needed before we could make anything of it. At the time Alton Reservoir was being built and they were dumping lorry loads of topsoil. I went to see one of the foremen, who agreed to help me. I told him where I wanted the soil and he asked me to pay the drivers £1 a load, cash in hand. This was great, as it solved my problem and helped them by avoiding long trips to dump the soil. So, under my direction, the loads started arriving and were tipped exactly where I asked, the drivers going away with an easy pint in their pockets. Once it was levelled, I had the start of my garden. British Rail had included a clause in the agreement that I should provide a five-strand wire fence to enclose my plot. There were many rolls of old, very tough galvanised signal wire discarded all over the yard and, together with a number of scrap barbed wire angle iron stakes from Wattisham, I soon put up the regulation fence. Without my knowledge, Pauline wrote to British Rail to say how much I had improved the land for them and suggested that they pay for the fence. They eventually agreed to pay for my materials and allowed me to claim £15 for my efforts.

As usual, there were duties to be done at Wattisham. At first I was put on the Orderly Sergeant Roster, requiring me to spend an occasional night on camp in the Sergeants' Mess to carry out the usual round of flag raising, mess complaints and the like. After a while however, the system was changed and I was put on the Duty Engineer Roster, still requiring me to stay in the Sergeants' Mess, but now I dealt with out-of-hours engineering matters such as supervising visiting aircraft requirements and having lists of people to call out when engineering problems arose and the station was closed down. Later I would also be trained as an MRD (Mobil Runway De-icer) operator, another duty, but luckily I was never called on to perform this. Someone had realised that the aircraft jets generated a lot of hot air and often blasted the ice and snow off the runway and taxiways as they taxied along or took off during the winter. A pair of jet engines were mounted on the front of a fuel tanker with the exhausts pointing forward and a control cabin mounted between the engines for the operator. Whenever clearance of ice and snow was required, a driver would control the tanker and the MRD Operator managed the jets, both interconnected with an intercom set. This was quite effective and saved the application of large amounts of chemical de-icer that caused harm to the environment, salt obviously not being an option close to aircraft.

I reported sick once again with a pain in my groin, and once again the MO diagnosed a hernia; he told me it was caused by smoking and advised me to give up right away. Puzzled, I asked him to explain, and he asked if I did heavy lifting in my job, to which I agreed. He said, 'You have been lifting something at some point and coughed at the same time, and the strain has caused the hernia. In a few days time you will wake up from the anaesthetic with a row of clips in your guts and if you cough it will cause you so much pain you will wish you had never, ever smoked!'

Needless to say, from that day to this, I have never smoked again. I was in the RAF Ely Hospital within two weeks, made a little easier this time as Pauline and the children could come and visit me. After the usual ten days there I was back at home on sick leave and soon ready for work again.

From the time of my arrival at Wattisham there had been talk of possible closure, but word came through that the squadrons would instead convert to Phantoms at some point. In order to keep the two phases apart I have written the next chapter separately to record the change. At the end of 1975 there were many changes afoot and the Lightning squadrons were moving, with aircraft coming and going in dribs and drabs, movements too complicated for me to recall. RAF Binbrook had been nominated to be the home of the Lightnings, but even after they left we were still 'Lightning Operational'. That is to say, we maintained the equipment and stocks of missiles at MSF and every once in a while a Lightning aircraft would be flown in for the procedures to be checked and training to be undertaken. This was particularly so during exercises, when our resources were tested and our preparedness for real emergencies measured.

And so the Lightnings eventually all left and most of the missiles were packed up and disposed of. But MSF was to have a revival and work started to convert our facilities for the new wave of equipment that was arriving.

12. Wattisham Phantoms

The first signs at MSF of the imminent arrival of Phantoms at Wattisham was the start of the works needed to accommodate the Sparrow and Sidewinder missiles that we would be handling. As these were American weapons, the procedures and equipment we used would be quite different and an intense period of training and preparation commenced.

The Sparrow is a semi-active radar guided weapon, it does not generate a radar signal but picks up a reflected radar signal from the target. That signal is transmitted by the parent aircraft and is known as illuminating the target; the parent aircraft continues to track the target until the missile strikes. The Phantom carries four Sparrow missiles in bays in the underside of the fuselage.

The Sidewinder is a heat seeking weapon similar to the Red Top and Firestreak. Once it acquires a target the weapon is fired and the parent aircraft breaks away. It was designed to use Nitrogen to cool the heat seeking head in the nose, but the RAF used the alternative pure air, utilising the facilities that were already in place for the Red Top. The Phantom carries four Sidewinders on underwing pylons, two launchers per pylon on each wing.

In the cathedral we had the pneumatic hoisting system extended to reach the area where the missiles would be unloaded. In the electronics workshop dedicated power and air supply points were fitted, two for the Sparrow testing equipment and two for Sidewinder testing. The pure air plant was modified and fitted with a cabinet we called the 'Iron Maiden'. This was a thick steel cabinet where the thin skinned Nitrogen bottles could be safely charged up to 3000 psi with pure air.

The new ground equipment was also issued to us; mobile assembly stands for the cathedral, Type S bomb trolleys and Sparrow/Sidewinder storage cradles for external transportation and storage. We also had an MJ4 loader for transferring the missiles on and off the Type S trolleys and storage racks. But before we received the test equipment we needed some training. I had been selected to manage the introduction of the new systems and together with two other plumbers, was sent on a Sparrow/Sidewinder course at RAF Coningsby. We travelled up by car and spent a very pleasant two weeks on the course learning all there was to know about our new missiles and the associated equipment. All work on the Sparrow and Sidewinder missiles is undertaken by plumbers and we needed to learn all the test and assembly procedures that we would be required to undertake.

I was given a room in the Sergeants' Mess and soon bumped into old friends and acquaintances in the bar and dining room. We had Wednesday afternoons off for sport and as the National Water Sports Centre wasn't too far away I had brought my water ski and a wetsuit with me just in case. I enjoyed two very pleasant afternoons there skiing on the purpose built ski lake and also on the bigger rowing lake, once the rowers had finished for the day. I got myself a meal on the way back to Coningsby and went to bed early after a drink in the bar, usually very tired by then.

Back at Wattisham we started to set up the assembly and test equipment, I was given the MSF armament inventory to manage and had complete control over all the equipment on the site. The test equipment was set up, two Sparrow test sets with the associated stands and drip trays and a dedicated bench for two Sidewinder test sets that needed no stands. The 'Iron Maiden' was checked out and the first Nitrogen bottles filled with pure air. Then assembly and testing of the missiles commenced, building up the stocks for operational readiness.

Two Phantom Squadrons were resident at Wattisham in 1976, Nos 23 and 56 Squadrons they worked up in readiness for Missile Practice Camp (MPC) at RAF Valley. The squadrons took live Sparrow and Sidewinder missiles from Wattisham with them for the firing, making it a test of the complete system from getting the parts out of the boxes to striking the targets. A 23 Squadron aircraft flying against a pilotless drone on the Aberporth Range successfully fired the first Wattisham Sparrow in April of 1976. There were many other practice firings made without incident. Except for one particular occasion.

~ RAF Plumber ~

First Wattisham live Sparrow firing

One afternoon whilst one of the Squadrons were away at MPC a call came in to advise us that one of our Sidewinders had broken in half. The missile is made up of four tubular sections, guidance, target detector, warhead and motor, joined together with torque loaded clamping rings. We were advised by Strike Command HQ of a crack detection procedure that needed to be carried out on all the clamping rings before any further firings could take place. Being an enthusiast for interesting jobs I volunteered to hot foot it to RAF Valley, accompanied by another plumber, Cpl Paddy Patterson, travelling in a Mini Van with the necessary equipment. I called Pauline to let her know that I would not be home for tea (pity really because it was something quite tasty no doubt) and we headed off through the evening traffic to Valley. There was a reception party waiting for us there on arrival and they showed us where the missiles were stored. Working through the night we stripped tested and reassembled about twelve missiles, finishing around 0300 hours. Paddy and I found some transit accommodation and flopped down exhausted, with no washing kit or bedding. But no matter, next morning we got away from Valley once we were sure that we were no longer needed, making the long tiring trek back to Wattisham and a decent night's sleep.

I think the powers-that-be at Strike Command HQ must have made a note of my availability because on a number of occasions they asked me to undertake a few unusual tasks. The next task that came along was a flight to RAF Wildenrath escorting missiles in transit. It seems that two complete Phantom loads of missiles were required there in a hurry, for what reason I do not recall. It was decided that they would be transported ready assembled and the only way to do that was on Type S Bomb trolleys by air. Each Trolley can carry a layer of four Sparrows on the lower cradle and a layer of four Sidewinders on the upper cradle, making a complete set for a Phantom. We prepared two complete trolley loads, making very sure that all the restraining straps were in good condition and very tight. I was accompanied again by Paddy Patterson and on the appointed day we assisted the MAMs team to load the two trolleys into the C130 aircraft that had been flown in from RAF Lyneham.

Type S trolleys loaded with Sparrow and Sidewinder missiles

After the trolleys were securely, braked, chocked and cross chained to the floor to prevent movement, we donned our ear defenders and took our seats for the flight. Take off was a little worrying as the missile trolleys lurched back against the restraints, but all was well and we had an easy flight. At Wildenrath there was a party waiting to unload us and we were given ½ hour to wait for the return flight. Knowing Wildenrath well it was just time to get to the NAAFI to buy our stock of duty frees before getting back to the dispersal in time for the return trip. We were taking the empty trolleys back to Wattisham although the aircraft was only going to Lyneham. I had therefore arranged for an MT vehicle from Wattisham to meet us there in order to transport the trolleys back. Once we had landed we got the empty trolleys loaded in quick time, Paddy went to London on leave and I rode in the vehicle back to Wattisham, job done.

Missile Servicing Flight parties were always a time to look forward to and much effort went into the preparation in order to entertain the families and friends properly. Generally we had an annual summer barbecue at MSF and a Christmas party, sometimes at MSF but usually at a local venue. The barbecues were held in the ground equipment section with a large marquee erected on the hard standing outside and the two inner bays decorated up with parachutes and lights, one as a bar and the other as a dance area. Music was provided by Radio Wattisham's disco, one of the lads was a volunteer disc jockey there and got the kit free. We usually produced our own food and put on drinks of all types. The event was always free, as we had been saving up in the months before with profit from the MSF canteen and regular fund raising draws. The Station Commander and all the Officers in the chain of Command were invited through courtesy but rarely attended, knowing we were well tucked away out of sight in the woods. But everyone enjoyed themselves and I am glad that Pauline could drive and didn't drink at all, otherwise I think I would have spent the night 'on camp'.

I was again roped in for EOD work during exercises and was made a team leader on one of the shifts. This meant that I had a Land Rover, a radio and an assistant (usually another plumber) and were sent out and about under the direction of the designated Local Defence Commander. We spent much of the time driving around the station dealing with so called suspicious packages and dodging into shelters whenever an air raid or Nuclear, Biological, Chemical

(NBC) alert sounded. Most of these packages were often nothing other than a cardboard box with a label describing the device and an Umpire standing by to question us what action we would take if it had been real bomb. On one occasion, we were on the other side of the airfield looking for a reported UXB when the radio asked if we could attend to another device. As we were busy at the time we advised that we were not in the vicinity of this new incident and asked the controller to call up another team. This let us off the hook for awhile and enabled us to complete what we were doing, picking the choice mushrooms that were growing in that part of the airfield and which later we shared with all the lads.

Our normal working hours were 0800 to 1200 hours and 1300 to 1700 hours five days a week. A source of interest to a number of us in the lunch hour was the nearby scrap dump, RAF scrap dumps contain all manner of useful items. A fellow SNCO, Sgt Dick Harvey spent most of his lunchtime at the dump salvaging copper wire that he sold to the local scrap metal dealer. Being a DIY enthusiast improving an old house, I carted home some useful items. The first large item was a carpet that I adapted to fit the dining room, then I found a very nice old-fashioned brass and china door bell push that fitted my front door. I still have a plastic fire bucket, and managed to build two complete sheds from wood, aluminium angle, discarded sheets of steel and corrugated asbestos. Another pursuit was wood collection. I had installed a wood burning central heating boiler at Delphis that needed constant feeding and I was always on the look out for fuel. I had bought an old pick-up truck and a new chain saw and got permission to take home any fallen trees that were in the woods to supplement what I found in the scrap dump. When I could I went to the swimming pool at lunch times, there were usually only swimmers doing lengths and I often managed to swim up to a mile before having to return to work.

The runway was to be closed at Wattisham for six months and the aircraft operated from RAF Wethersfield in Essex for the duration. The QRA facility would also be operated from Wethersfield and the squadrons would remain operational. It was necessary for us to transport enough missiles and equipment there in support of this move and it was decided that everything would be transported by road. For the duration of the detachment there was much movement between the bases, apart from flying, all other aspects of Wattisham would continue and enough missiles had been transported and stored at Wethersfield. A few MSF personnel went on permanent detachment there but every day a working party left MSF to work at Wethersfield for the day.

My role was to work between the two bases, depending on the task in hand. However, there was suddenly an urgent need to transport two complete Type S trolley loads of Sparrows and Sidewinders there and once again a C130 was called up. Having been through the routine once before this was much easier and we soon got airborne. The flight time to Wethersfield was ten minutes, but to my surprise there was even in-flight catering. As soon as we were off the ground the Air Loadmaster dished out cups of coffee and a biscuit while we peered through the small windows seeking familiar sights. The return trip was easy; we brought some empty trolleys back to Wattisham, again with in-flight catering available, a very nice day out and again, job done.

The only other flight I got while at Wattisham was in a single engine side-by-side two seat Bulldog trainer with a large clear canopy. The University Air Squadrons visited Wattisham for their summer camps and brought a number of Bulldogs for the students to continue their training in the unfamiliar territory. When not in use by the students the instructors would take station personnel up for a trip and a waiting list was kept with telephone numbers. I just got my name onto the quickly filled list one day and eventually late in the morning I got a call. I was kitted up with a parachute and instructed on the safety procedures and crash landing drill before we took off. The pilot instructor asked me where I wanted to go; I explained roughly where I lived and a few navigational marks and we took off on the main runway. The first point was Hadleigh and then following the old Hadleigh to Bentley railway line until we hit the main line at Bentley. I asked the pilot to turn right down the valley and when we passed over my house he flew up and down for a few minutes. After awhile Pauline came out in the garden waving her arms because she guessed it was me and it was always our practice to wave at passing aircraft. On the way back the pilot asked if I fancied a few aerobatics to which I agreed. Close to Hadleigh he climbed up above the thin broken cloud and dived down through a wide hole into a complete loop, practically over the town. At Wattisham we did a few roller landings on the runway and the grass eventually doing the final landing on grass. To me, it had been one of the most exciting days of my life, particularly the loop. The only regret was that I hadn't had my camera with me, you have to pay a fortune for aerial photographs of your house.

By now I was MSF Site Supervisor, running the day to day operations of MSF from the MSF Control Room outside the wire. Strike Command HQ came up with some more jobs for me that broke the routine, one was to spend ten days at Strike Command HQ at High Wycombe writing new servicing schedules and generally helping out while they were short of staff in the AAGW office. The other task was a week at RAF Coningsby undertaking an audit of servicing procedures, a job that made me very unpopular with the senior permanent staff there. But it was all part of making the Phantom force more efficient and standardising practices in the different MSF locations.

MSF Control – l to r WO Tom Cox, Flt Lt Bob Appleyard, Author

Every once in a while we had a Taceval (Tactical Evaluation) exercise, a major Strike Command test of the station's ability to go to war at short notice. We never knew when this would commence, usually about once a year and called at any time of the day or night. It would be a major call out for the whole station and led right up to live missile firings by the squadrons. As usual, I was involved in incidents that needed some expertise. On one Taceval a call came in that a Phantom taxiing with a live Sidewinder had a missile guidance failure and the squadron plumbers were waiting for a replacement to be delivered asap. Paddy and I jump into a Land Rover, loaded a Type S Trolley with a set of four live Sidewinders and headed out to the dispersal area. There we found the aircraft with the crew strapped in, the engines running at 10% and two plumbers waiting for our assistance. There was no waiting around, the four of us unloaded the offending missile from the launcher on the pylon and loaded on one of the new ones we had brought. After a few seconds the pilot signalled that all was well and taxied off for a successful firing, again job done. Unfortunately, whereas everyone had a pair of ear defenders to wear, I did not. The consequences of which were that I suffered from tinnitus. I had already lost a lot of my high pitch hearing from other RAF induced noises but now I had permanent singing in my ears, a condition that I have had to live with ever since.

Just after that it was decided that a weapons controller would be based in the main operations control room during all alerts to ensure the continuity of weapons delivery and movement. I was one of two MSF Ch/Ts to undertake this role, maintaining radio contact with the squadrons, MSF and the weapons delivery teams. In the operations bunker we sat in front of a large map of the airfield mounted on a magnetic board and showing all the resources available to the commanders. I devised a system of magnetic tiles denoting all the various weapon loads that we had available and worked up the operating procedures we would use. Although this was an interesting task, I did not really want to be stuck for 12 hours a day underground and was quite pleased when my shift ended. The radio call sign of Ducal had been allocated to the MSF network, Ducal Sunray being the MSF Flight Commander in the MSF control, I was Ducal 1, and all the delivery Land Rovers Ducal 2, Ducal 3 and so on. Although there is a strict procedure for talking over the radio, a little light-hearted banter often crept in. I gradually corrupted the Ducal call sign to Dougal, as it sounded very similar, and this lead to odd unofficial references to Zebedee, Mr MacHenry and Ermintrude from the lads on the other end of the radios, much to the annoyance of the powers that may be listening in. We were occasionally chastised for this, but it was difficult to stop and was just a bit of fun to break the routine.

In April 1982 the Falklands war flared up and we were advised that we would be supplying Sidewinder missiles for the Harrier Force that would be travelling there. We started to do a major servicing on all the missiles that would be transported on the Navy Task Force. Eventually we were given a deadline for completion and transportation by road to the docks, a task that was left to the MSF WO and I to organise. Forty-eight hours before the deadline expired I got the inevitable telephone call from Strike Command HQ. The problem they had was that if the Harriers got to the Falklands and were transferred to a land base, there would be no supporting pure air supply for the missiles. It would mean that the Nitrogen bottles would have to be transferred to the aircraft carriers by helicopter on a daily basis for recharging. The question I was asked was 'If I was given a mobile pure air plant, could I modify it within twenty-four hours to be used in the Falklands for Nitrogen bottle charging'? I was stumped for a moment, not knowing what the plant was like, what outlets it had and all the finer detail I needed. As I was being pressed and knowing my ability to get things done under pressure, I stuck my neck out and agreed.

The ball started rolling immediately and within a few hours an Army Land Rover arrived with two pongos and a pure air plant mounted on a trailer. This was a standard piece of kit for the Army who used it for charging pure air into some pieces of their heat sensing field equipment. They gave me a crash course on the capabilities and operation of the machine and left. I worked for the rest of the day and late into the evening modifying the outlets and connecting up stainless steel pipes with our own connectors. The next thing was to devise some form of protection system for the operator. We normally put the long thin walled Nitrogen bottles into our Iron Maiden and shut the doors while charging. At the station workshops I found they had some mild steel piping just big enough to slide the bottles in for protection. One of the NCOs hacked off two lengths of the piping for me and the job was nearly done. Quite late at night I did a complete test of the system by charging up two bottles to the requisite 3000psi and taking a note of the time taken and the procedure I had used. I'd had a few sharp words with some of the uncooperative people I needed to deal with during the day and this was one of those days when I was glad to get home and get some rest.

Author receiving AOCs Commendation December 1982

The next morning I telephoned Strike Command and advised them that the job was complete and they could have the machine back. That was when they told me the second part of the deal; they wanted one of our corporals to be trained to use the machine and to travel to the Falklands with the Task Force. I am not sure how he was selected but Cpl Martin Thorne was nominated for the job and I gave him as much training as I could in the next few hours. He was married with a small son, lived close by and was given a few hours off to prepare his kit before he had to leave. He set off with a supply of spare parts and our very good wishes; from what we eventually heard he successfully completed the job and worthily represented MSF Wattisham in the Falklands. While he was away I visited his wife and son regularly, keeping them in touch with the MSF family, and she told me of his news that arrived rather spasmodically in his letters.

We continued to support the Falklands Task Force, the results of which are now written into history. But it was now time for me to leave RAF Wattisham. After 30 years in the service, my time was up and I was due for demob.

For the record, I received three AOC's Commendations while at MSF, dated 1 January 1977, 17 June 1979 and 31 December 1982 and in 1978 I was awarded my Long Service and Good Conduct medal for 25 years of undetected crime.

I finally left Wattisham on 23 May 1983. My contract was up and it was time for me to try my hand at other things.

13. Who needs a civvy armourer?

When I arrived at RAF Wattisham in 1974 I knew I only had another nine years to serve, as I had extended my period of engagement until the age of 47 years. This was a standard point to leave the RAF, the next point being at age 55 years. However, I had seen too many people leave the service at that age and not last very long in their new life before having problems like heart attacks, depression and the like. I had also realised that it would be easier to get a job at age of 47 years than it would at 55; there weren't many people around who wanted to employ an old civvy armourer trained in AAGW and EOD.

So I decided to restart my programme of taking GCE 'O' levels again and completed an evening class in Chemistry at Suffolk College in Ipswich, gaining a pass in June 1979. The following year RAF Wattisham put on a crash weekend course in Commerce with the aim of taking the O-level exam. It was only open to those with Maths and English O-level certificates and was run by a specialist tutor hired by the Education Section. We had classes on Friday evening and all day Saturday and Sunday and were given lectures in Commerce for half of the time while the rest of the sessions were taken up by answering old O-level question papers. The theory was that 75% of the questions came up in some form in every Commerce paper that was set and we would receive enough knowledge to pass. This was quite justified as I gained a pass in November 1980. I took a similar weekend crash course in Economics the following year and gained a pass in June 1981.

Around this time, RAF Wattisham was fitted out with a Prime mainframe computer and two terminals were located in the MSF HQ building. Although this was only a trial, secret information such as missile stocks was not allowed on the machine. But it was useful for finding spare parts and interrogating lists of defects etc. However, the interesting thing that I found was that it could be programmed in Basic Language to do simple functions. At the same time the Education Section started a series of Computer Studies classes aimed at preparation for the O-level examination. I soon signed up for this and thoroughly enjoyed the new challenges that it gave me. The finale of the course was to undertake a project to be submitted as part of the exam and I decided to put together a programme that would assist with AAGW servicing.

Although details about the operational live missiles were secret, we also had a wide range of acquisition, training, drill (inert) and ballast missiles that were carried on the aircraft and these all needed regular servicing. These details were not classified as secret and were ideal for my project. If the programme was successful it could eventually be used in a situation where secret information involving live missile details was recorded on dedicated standalone machines. I had to learn Basic programming from a book and spent hours and hours of my spare time at MSF and at home, writing and testing the programme. When I was on MSF Duty Fitter I stayed up until the early hours of the morning, perfecting and modifying my work.

The aim was to produce a programme that would self-update on a daily basis and call forward missiles for servicing when due. It was also required to provide a history sheet for every component and groups of assembled components or missiles that could be extracted and printed out when required. Finally, it needed to provide a screen display for each missile when called up by serial number. I eventually achieved all of the aims and produced my project folder for submission at the time of the exam. Just before leaving Wattisham in May 1983 I received my Grade B O-level in Computer Studies, giving me a total of 10 GCE O-levels to back my quest for a job when I finally left.

I also decided to have a medical opinion about my hearing before I left the service. Although my hearing was good, I had lost some of my ability to hear the upper range of sounds and the tinnitus was still with me. The MO agreed that I should have a check at the RAF Hospital at Ely and I went along for an appointment with a Group Captain hearing specialist. He gave me a thorough examination of the ears, did several tests and advised me of his findings. He said, 'Chief you and I are both getting on now and like me you should be in the Shetlands where it is nice and quiet, tending the sheep'. In other words, there was nothing that could be done and I would have to live with it.

A few months before I was due to leave I was offered promotion to Flight Sergeant and I had to make a decision whether to accept or not. The problem I faced was that the promotion was dependent upon posting to RAF Leeming in Yorkshire and it would also require me to extend my service to age 55. Pauline and I had a long discussion about this dilemma and I came to the conclusion that I would turn the offer down. There were a number of reasons for this. Firstly, for the sake of my family, I would have to live away during the week and travel home at weekends, but the increase in pay would only cover my travel costs. Moving was not a very good option as far as we were concerned because it would be very disruptive for our family. Secondly, there was no increase in the rate of pension between Ch/T and Flt Sgt and I would need to achieve WO rank before getting any increase at retirement. Finally, I had always aimed at leaving at the age of 47 years for the health and employment reasons given above.

The RAF provided support for those retiring after a lengthy period of service and the first thing I did was to go on a one-day course for SNCOs in London. This was to provide us with basic information about pensions, trade unions, keeping fit in retirement, second careers and producing a Curriculum Vitae etc. This part was very useful and on my return I set about writing my CV and getting 100 copies professionally printed.

This is what I produced: –

CURRICULUM VITAE: MICHAEL JOHN ANDERTON

Born: 11.7.36. Married with 2 dependent children.
Address: 'Delphis', Station Road, Bentley, Ipswich IP9 2DB. Tel. Ipswich 310014.

EDUCATION AND QUALIFICATIONS

Colchester Royal Grammar School aged 12 to 16. Joined the Royal Air Force (RAF). Qualified as Armament Fitter after 3 year apprenticeship. Passed promotion exams for Corporal, Sergeant and Chief Technician. From 1969 to 1982 passed GCE O Level English, Mathematics, General

Paper, Physics, Geography, Geometrical and Mechanical Drawing, Commerce, Economics and Chemistry. Currently studying Computer Studies. In 1976 passed RAF Management course.

CAREER IN RAF
Leaving RAF after 30 year engagement with the rank of Chief Technician (for 11 years.) Awarded 3 commendations whilst in final post (8 years)

EXPERIENCE
Management. For the past 8 years I have been the Senior Supervisor of a guided missile section of up to 40 men. I have been responsible for organising and planning the work routine. I supervise a central control and records section co-ordinating all activities internal and external to the section, a fleet of 7 vehicles and the associated ground equipment. I am often required to advise higher authority and attend meetings on behalf of my immediate superiors.

Administration. As a Senior Supervisor I supervise the updating of personnel and technical records. The dissemination of incoming and outgoing mail up to secret level. Progression of equipment requirements including receipts and despatch of explosives and secret stores. Drafting of minor letters and reports to higher authority. Operation of a filing system up to secret level. Amendment of manuals and the operation of a VDU computer terminal. I control a large inventory of stores and equipment.

Projects. During the past 8 years I have been responsible for the development of modifications, research, trials and quality assurance on missiles and associated handling equipment.

Technical. During my service I have carried out handling, storage and preparation for use of many types of explosive and armament equipment. The servicing, modification and rectification of aircraft equipment. Bomb Disposal duties and as an instructor in ejection seat safety and also bomb loading techniques.

GENERAL
I am a Parent Governor and Correspondent to the Governors of the local Primary School. I am on the local Playing Field Committee. I have lived and worked in Singapore, Malta, Germany and Cyprus. I enjoy swimming and any outdoor activities as a means of keeping fit. I am an avid do-it-yourself enthusiast.

AIM
I aim to use my total experience to start a second career as a civilian.

The RAF allowed either a resettlement course in any selected subject or a six week attachment with a prospective employer; this meant I was available to start work any time from the middle of May. With my CV in hand I started applying for jobs, and soon got an interview with Cookson and Zinn at Hadleigh. They needed a Transport Manager to organise contract hauliers to transport the very large storage tanks that they manufactured. I attended the interview with the works manager in my uniform straight from work, and after a tour of the works and a thorough interview, I was offered the post. This was great and just what I needed, however, just after I got home there was a call from the works manager. He advised me that they had interviewed another candidate with plenty of experience and regretfully had to turn me down.

I managed to get several more interviews with the likes of British Telecom, Suffolk Coastal District Council, and, after passing the Civil Service exam, with Customs and Excise, but all to no avail. Finally, I opted for an attachment with a local employer. Three friends of mine in Bentley had started a small business manufacturing modelling paints, working from an industrial unit in Lawford near Manningtree. They agreed to take me on unpaid for six weeks with the prospect of being employed as the General Manager at the end of the period.

The Compucolor logo

The company was called Compucolor and sold small tins of paint in any colour you could describe. They had a range that covered every type of aircraft, railway engine, boat and vehicle there had ever been. If a customer required a colour that was not in the range they could match it with a colour scanner and computer programme that provided the mixing details of the ingredients required. A batch was then mixed to that specification.

So for the final six weeks of my service I would be working as a civilian and all that was required now was to organise a demob party at MSF. Dick Harvey and I were both due to leave at the same time and agreed that we would combine our efforts. It was usual for the person leaving the service to provide all the food and drink and the people who would be left behind to have a collection for a leaving gift and to carry out some form of leaving ceremony. Dick and I bought in large quantities of beer in cans and a few soft drinks and paid Hazel our friendly civilian cleaner to organise the food. So on the afternoon of 23 May 1983 we had our 'do'. At the end of the party the boss, Flt Lt Bob Appleyard, gave a speech and made the presentations. Dick and I were then loaded aboard a flat top trolley and towed by all the lads around MSF before being finally ejected through the gates.

And that was the end of my 30 years as a RAF plumber.

Ejected from MSF after 30 years of service

14. Epilogue

At Compucolor I got heavily involved in the business, attending trade fairs and exhibitions, designing and manufacturing paint display stands and dealing with the postal orders that poured in. I had thought that this was a chance to make a million, the three directors had expansion plans ready once they had become properly established and I would be part of it. But all was not well and there was no volume of orders coming in and the company could not afford to pay me. Gradually we lost money, eventually going into receivership within a few months of me joining. I signed on for unemployment benefit and started looking for a steady job.

However, I soon had a successful interview with Suffolk County Council's Highways Department, was appointed as a Rights of Way Assistant and started work with a permanent contract on 12 December 1983. I was based in St Edmund House in Ipswich on work involving the management of Public Rights of Way across the county. I was soon an expert in dealing with problems associated with Public Footpaths, Bridleways and all the highways of the countryside.

After about a year the department was reorganised and I was appointed as the Central Area Rights of Way Warden based at the Great Blakenham depot. I was now much more involved in enforcement and other legal issues connected with the path network, but now covering the central part of the county.

An ex 74th Entry armourer, Roger Martin, also worked in the Highways Department and in April 1988 we travelled down to RAF Halton for the 35th anniversary of our entry into the service. There we met a number of other ex-74th Entry apprentices, including my old friend Graham Napthen (Mothballs). We were given the place of honour behind the pipe band to proudly march down to workshops at the head of all the trainees. We then split up into various trades groups to tour the workshops and schools areas before completing this nostalgic day.

74th Entry plumbers reunion, Author first left, Mothballs with beard

Although I enjoyed Rights of Way work, especially being out and about every day, the legal and enforcement side of the work was sometimes a bit stressful. In 1988 the County Council's Planning Department was about to set up a new jointly funded Countryside Commission project to promote the Rights of Way network as a recreational amenity and I applied for the post.

With my new found experience, I was successfully appointed and started work in August 1988, this time based in the Planning Department back at St Edmund House. The job title was Countryside Access Project Officer and over the next eleven years I developed and managed the project until 2000. Unfortunately, the contract was only for three years initially because of the uncertain availability of Countryside Commission funding. But over the years I managed to get this renewed on a regular basis. I had a team of two assistants and a reasonable budget and we set about producing circular walks with descriptive leaflets. We also encouraged parish councils and village people to do the same thing, and later provided funding for them to undertake some maintenance of the footpaths themselves.

Countryside Access Project Officer 1988

In my spare time I had been writing a weekly walk in the Saturday Edition of the Ipswich Evening Star newspaper and later produced a booklet of 12 walks for them. The weekly articles continued until 2000 by which time the number of books I had written had reached four. I had also produced a book of 30 walks for a national publisher entitled Teashop Walks in Suffolk. My own website entitled Suffolk Country Walks was also now available with walks for the public to download. This led to Anglia Railways (now called One) asking me to produce walks from their Suffolk stations for publication on their website, this resulted in another series of 20 walks.

Countryside Access Project Officer 1998

Retired 2000

~ RAF Plumber ~

All this time I was still managing the Countryside Access Project but in 1999 the money from the Countryside Agency, as it was now called, was to be drastically cut and some savings had to be made. I devised a plan that would enable the County Council to maintain the level of service that we had provided but without a project officer at the helm. For me it would mean redundancy a year before I was due to finally retire, a scheme I looked forward to. The powers-that-be agreed to this and I left the County Council on 10 July 2000 after 17 years of service.

In retirement I continued to produce walk articles and self-published a book entitled Suffolk Town Trails describing a walk around all 20 of Suffolk's towns. I continue to send a walk a month in for publication in the East Anglian Daily Times Suffolk magazine. I still maintain my walks website and now also manage the Bentley Parish Council website. I was clerk to the parish council for seven years and am now secretary/treasurer of the Bentley Improvement Group, receiving Landfill tax money for distribution to worthy environmental causes around the village. I have also recently become secretary/treasurer of the Bentley Parish Plan Group.

I have continued to have an interest in computers. At Suffolk County Council I obtained a European Computer Driving Licence, a British Computer Society qualification, and now have a broadband wireless network in my office at home.

We eventually moved from Delphis to a small bungalow at 1 The Link in Bentley. However, this was only a stepping stone to a larger bungalow. We were to arrange a part-exchange deal with a lady who lived at 26 West Mill Green, Bentley and who wanted a smaller house. This was an area that I had always had an ambition to live in and an added bonus for me was that it is only 200 yards from the Case is Altered pub.

Finally, I have got the bungalow, garden and five grandchildren to keep me busy. I receive pensions from the RAF, Suffolk County Council and the government to make life quite pleasant. And who knows, perhaps one day one of my grandchildren will also become a RAF plumber?

Suffolk Country Walks books

Books published
Suffolk Country Walks Book 1 – Evening Star
Suffolk Country Walks Book 2 – Evening Star
Suffolk Country Walks Book 3 – Evening Star
Suffolk Country Walks Book 4 – Evening Star
Tea Shop walks in Suffolk – Sigma Press
Suffolk Town Trails – Suffolk Country Walks

Websites
Suffolk Country Walks – **http://www.anderton.btinternet.co.uk**
Bentley Suffolk – **http://www.bentley.suffolk.gov.uk**

Glossary

7 store carrier – bomb carrier capable of holding 7 X 1000lb bombs
20 mm Hispano – type of aircraft gun
AAGW – Air to Air Guided Weapons
Air Loadmaster – aircraft cabin crew
Air Quarter Master – former name for Air Loadmaster
Allen Scythe – petrol driven undergrowth cutting machine
Alvis trolley – Canberra bomb loader
AMQ – Airman's Married Quarter
Andover – twin engine turbo-prop aircraft
AOC – Air Officer Commanding
APC - Armament Practice Camp
Acquisition missile – dummy missile that locks onto a target
ASF – Aircraft Servicing Flight, usually based in a hanger
Astra Cinema – RAF chain of cinemas
ATC – Air Traffic Control
ATAF – Allied Tactical Air Force
A.Tech(W) – Aircraft Technician (Weapons)
Ballast missile – missile shaped balancing weight
Basic – first phase of training
BD – Bomb Disposal
Bed pack – blankets and sheets folded in a neat bundle
Beverley – large four piston engine heavy transport aircraft
BFG - British Forces in Germany
Big Bertha – large German gun
Boggies - national servicemen
Bomb beam – bomb carrying section of Canberra bomb bay
Bondu Basher – Renault 4
Bull – bullshit, spit and polish, cleaning
Bulldog - single piston engine side by side two seat trainer aircraft
Bunk – single man room
Brass - senior officers
Brats – apprentices
Breech – firing chamber of gun
Britannia - four engine turbo-prop passenger aircraft
C130 – Hercules four engine turbo-prop transport aircraft

Canberra – twin engine bomber and photo reconnaissance aircraft
Chief – see Ch/T
Chit - note
Ch/T – Chief Technician
Civvies – civilian clothing or civilian people
CO – Commanding Officer
Conical support spring – used to hold detonator against the firing pin
Coolies – civilian labour force
Corporal of Horse – Army SNCO rank
Cpl – Corporal
Cpl/T – Corporal Technician
CTC – Carbon Tetra Chloride
DA - Duty Armourer
Deep Sea Box – packing case for personal kit
Defaulters – airmen on punishment duty
Demob – demobilisation, leaving the RAF
Dhobi wallers – laundry workers
Dolphin kick – leg movement in butterfly stroke
Dove – small twin piston engine passenger aircraft
Drill (store) – inert or dummy for training etc.
End Ex – End of Exercise
EOD – Explosive Ordnance Disposal
Erks – lower ranks
ESA – Explosives Storage Area
Fairies - instrument fitters
FEAF – Far East Air Force
Firesteak - heat seeking AAGW
Form 295 – leave pass
Form 1250 – RAF identity card
Flt Lt – Flight Lieutenant
Flt Sgt - Flight Sergeant
Flight – a group of service men or aircraft
Freight fit – fitted out to carry freight
Fusing – fitting detonators, fuzes, tail units and safety devices etc.
GCE – General Certificate of Education
Gen App – General Application form
Genned up – studied
GPO – General Post Office
GSM – General Service Medal
Hanger – large building to house aircraft
Harmonisation – aligning guns and gunsight on a fixed point

~ RAF Plumber ~

Harrier – vertical take off and landing single jet engine fighter aircraft
Hastings – four piston engine transport aircraft
HE – High Explosive
Head sharpened – hair cut
Heavies - engine fitters
Hercules – see C130
Heron – small four piston engine light passenger aircraft
Hiring – civilian house hired by the RAF
HK – Hong Kong
Hunter- single jet engine fighter
Hydraburner – heavy duty petrol cooker
Iron Maiden – cabinet for charging nitrogen cylinders
i/c – in charge
IED – Improvised Explosive Device
Indulgence flight – free passage on an aircraft
IWM – Imperial War Museum
Jet provost – twin seat single jet engine training aircraft
J/T - Junior Technician
LABS – Low Altitude Bombing System
LAC – Leading Aircraftsman
Lightning – twin jet engine fighter aircraft
Loadmaster – see Air Loadmaster
MAMs – Mobile Air Movements
Magirus Deutz truck – German built 3-ton truck
Maria Theresa Thaler - silver coin used for trading by Arabs
Master Engineer – Engineer of WO rank
Matelots or matey-lots – sailors
MJ-4 – Phantom equipment loader
MO – Medical Officer
MPC – Missile Practice Camp
MRD – Mobile Runway De-icer
MSF – Missile Servicing Flight
MT – Motor Transport
MU – Maintenance Unit
Muzzle – open end of barrel
NAAFI – Navy Army Air Force Institute, canteens and shops
NBC - Nuclear, Biological, Chemical
NCO – Non Commissioned Officer
Nissen hut – round roof corrugated sheet building
OCU – Operational Conversion Order
OS – Orderly Sergeant

~ *RAF Plumber* ~

Pembroke – small twin piston engine general purpose aircraft
Phantom – twin jet engine fighter bomber aircraft
Pick up taxis – taxis that pick up other passengers along the route
Plumbers – armourers
Pongos - army personnel
POSB or Pos-Bee - Post Office Savings Bank
QRA - Quick Reaction Alert
RAAF – Royal Australian Air Force
Red Top – heat seeking AAGW
RNZAF – Royal New Zealand Air Force
Russian Bears – Russian bomber aircraft
SABT – Standard Airfield Bomb Transporter
SAC – Senior Aircraftsman
Safety equipment – parachutes, dinghies and associated harnesses
SAP – Semi Armour Piercing
SAR – Search and Rescue
Second line – second level of servicing
Sgt – Sergeant
Shinys - administrative staff
SHQ – Station Headquarters
Sidewinder – American heat seeking AAGW
Signal pistol – signal flare gun
SNCO – Senior NCO
Snowdrops - RAF police
Sortie - flight of a combat aircraft on a mission
Sparkys – electricians
Sparrow – American semi-active radar AAGW
Square rig – navy uniform with bell bottoms
Squadron – group of Flights
Squint and Squeeze – rifle shooting
SSQ - Station Sick Quarters
Station Armoury – main armament building of RAF station
Steelies - fighter pilots
Strike – raid
Taceval - Tactical Evaluation
TAF – Transit Aircraft Flight
Taxi dancing – buying tickets to dance with the establishment girls
TD21 - Training Directive 21
Thaler – see Maria Theresa Thaler
Tinnitus – singing noise in the ears
Tombola – bingo

~ RAF Plumber ~

Type F trolley – elderly bomb transporting trailer
Type S trolley – modern extendable bomb transporting trailer
Type R loader – small single bomb loading machine
USAAF – United States Army Air Force
V1 Doodlebug – German flying bomb
V2 Rocket – German bomb delivered by rocket
Varsity – twin piston engine aircrew training aircraft
VC10 – four jet engine passenger aircraft
Venom – single jet engine, single seat fighter bomber with twin tail booms
Viscount – four engine turbo-prop airliner
WCSWSC - Western Cyprus Services Water Ski Club
Whirlwind – helicopter used for SAR
WO – Warrant Officer
WRAF – Women's Royal Air Force
Wren – Women's Royal Naval Service
Wing – a group of Squadrons
Zobs - officers